Liturgy and Justice

Liturgy and Justice
To Worship God in Spirit and Truth

Anne Y. Koester
Editor

THE LITURGICAL PRESS
Collegeville, Minnesota

www.litpress.org

Cover design by Greg Becker.

1	2	3	4	5	6	7	8

Library of Congress Cataloging-in-Publication Data

Notre Dame Center for Pastoral Liturgy. Conference (29th : 2001)
    Liturgy and justice : to worship God in spirit and truth / Anne Y. Koester, editor.
      p. cm.
    Includes bibliographical references.
    ISBN 0-8146-2791-9 (alk. paper)
      1. Catholic Church—Liturgy—Congresses.   2. Christianity and justice—Catholic Church—Congresses.   I. Koester, Anne Y. II. Title.

BX1970.A1 N68 2001
264'.02—dc21

                                   2002069547

To
the courageous pioneers of liturgical and social renewal,
past, present, and future.

Contents

Introduction

From June 18–21, 2001, the Notre Dame Center for Pastoral Liturgy hosted its twenty-ninth annual pastoral liturgy conference. The theme of the conference, "Liturgy and Justice: To Worship God in Spirit and Truth," reflects the Center's conviction that the intrinsic relationship between liturgy and justice is critical to the ongoing renewal of Church life and the created world. As the papers presented at the conference and included in this volume indicate, liturgical celebrations and the work of justice are tightly woven threads of the same cloth. In other words, gathering to worship and striving for justice are not separate compartments or unrelated endeavors in the Christian life; rather, liturgy and justice together are constitutive of and expressive of the Church itself. Quite simply, authentic discipleship demands that the already existing relationship between our liturgy and our mission as ministers of justice be *lived*. Full, conscious, and active participation in the liturgy is a continuous engagement, which compels us, stretches us, and empowers us to be full, conscious, and active servants of justice. And as ministers of justice, we must risk being broken open and transformed by the experience of liturgy. We must allow the ritual and the power of the Church at prayer to shape our hearts, nourish our spirits, and direct our journeys.

The shared concerns of liturgy and justice are many. The presenters and participants at the pastoral liturgy conference brought several of these intersections—where the concerns of liturgy and justice meet—to the foreground, where questions could be asked, challenges named, insights appropriated, and hopes expressed. The goal of the conference was to increase awareness of the profound nature of the liturgy-justice relationship and of the potential it holds for contemporary times. Indeed, its inherent potential needs to be realized in our day.

Gilbert Ostdiek, O.F.M., opened the conference with a keynote address that lifted up several of the pioneers of the twentieth-century American liturgical and social movements—Virgil Michel, O.S.B., Dorothy Day, Gerald Ellard, Catherine de Hueck Doherty, H. A. Reinhold, and many others. This generation of courageous and faithful Christians responded to life, including the social injustices of the day, by looking through a liturgical lens. They could not imagine the liturgical and social renewal efforts as separate, unrelated dimensions of the Christian life. Ostdiek urges that we honor the pioneers by following their example and by acting upon the legacy with which we have been entrusted: "The vision they have left us is breathtaking. . . . It is not something already completed; rather, it is a task given over to us to carry out again in our day. It is a legacy whose doing awaits us. And surely there is much to be done, in ways great and small, to re-weave liturgy and justice, and indeed all the ministries, once more into a seamless whole."

The next two general session speakers at the 2001 conference exemplify what it means to embrace the legacy Father Ostdiek described. Eleanor Josaitis, cofounder and executive director of Focus: HOPE, a civil and human rights organization in Detroit, shares her own inspirational story. Her journey in life led her to become active in a grassroots movement that grew into an outreach organization recognized worldwide for the solutions it has found to the problems of racism, poverty, and injustice. Monsignor William Linder, founder of New Community Corporation (NCC) in Newark, describes the many significant contributions NCC has made and continues to make to the community. NCC came to be when in July of 1967, members of an African American parish in Newark felt compelled to respond to civil disorder and violence in their neighborhood. "The parish took a firm stand," he said, "making it clear that the Church must make a positive response to the cries of the people." Ms. Josaitis and Monsignor Linder testify to the ideal that the reign of God is rehearsed when we build just communities.

In the final general session, Walter J. Burghardt, S.J., addressed the critical need for liturgy and justice to be reunited. His approach is one that links liturgy with biblical justice and therefore, with all of our relationships. Burghardt reminds us: "We are servants of justice—but only if we do not sever social action from the most powerful source of grace at our command," that is, the liturgy. He also insists that "social activists and practitioners of God's justice on the one hand, and liturgists and worshipers at God's liturgy on the other hand, dare not constitute two utterly separate organizations." Only by drawing together the liturgists and social reformers can the "body of Christ move more effectively from church to world, from altar to people, from Christ crucified on Calvary to Christ crucified at the crossroads of our earth."

The workshop sessions of the conference offered participants the opportunity to receive and share information on various issues of social concern, exchange ideas for how to relate these issues to what we do in liturgy, and conceive ways of forming the Christian faithful in the liturgy-justice relationship.

One such workshop session focused on the increasingly important topic of globalization. John P. Hogan approaches the issue of globalization from a eucharistic perspective. He asks, "How does the Eucharist call us to stewardship and global solidarity with the poor?" In response, Hogan proposes "an understanding of Eucharist with a corresponding discernment process that allows, even compels, the believing community to become aware, get involved, and exert influence on the globalization problematic." The Eucharist, he argues, "provides the identity and work plan for us as a Church to travel the path of conversion, communion, and solidarity with the poor."

Brother David Andrews, C.S.C., urges us to be mindful of the relationship between liturgy and the social issues that impact rural life. In particular, he encourages us to think about our tables—family tables, community tables, and faith tables—and to recall that the "intent of liturgy is to transform the world into a mirror of itself, a banquet of self-sacrificing love." He adds, "We shape each other and our world at our tables."

Zeni Fox explores the new leadership scene that has emerged in the Roman Catholic Church today, which brings both opportunities and challenges to the Church—a Church that has a commitment to justice as a central tenet. She proposes actions that are needed in response to these changes, actions that will enable us to build right relationships, and ultimately, empower us to bring forth a more just Church.

Frances B. O'Connor, C.S.C., considers whether there is justice for women in the Church's liturgy. She reports on her interviews of women in various countries and discusses her findings that women around the world often feel excluded from full participation in ministry and in the liturgy. She then comments on what women might teach liturgists about injustices and suggests how liturgists might respond.

Two of the workshop sessions focused on the experiences of particular cultures within the U.S. Church and the need for understanding these cultures in order for there to be justice within the Church and the broader community. Daniel Lizárraga encourages dialogue on matters pertaining to the Latino experience in the U.S. In particular, he says an understanding of Latino culture can assist liturgists with providing for the initiation and formation of the faithful, as well as the enhancement of worship.

C. Vanessa White speaks to the experience of liturgy as a liberating force for African Americans. She explains the essential relationship between black spirituality and the experience of liturgy: "If liturgy does not address the Spirit of God, the Catholic faith, and the lived reality of black people (our spirituality), then liturgy will not have the power to transform and liberate."

Four conference workshops emphasized that key to sensitizing the Christian faithful to the liturgy-justice relationship is the promotion of catechesis and faith formation as being rooted in this very same relationship. Mary Alice Piil, C.S.J., encourages us to see the Church's spirituality—the liturgy—as a school of discipleship, that is, the source of direction for the Christian life. The liturgy, she says, expresses the reality of the Christian life, yet it is also the font from which we draw the strength necessary to live the paschal mystery in the modern world.

James M. Schellman advocates a vision of the process of Christian initiation as one that brings us to full stature in Christ and equips us, as the Body of Christ, to be a leaven in the world, transforming it into a place of justice and peace. He suggests possibilities for mission-centered catechumenal formation—in the word, liturgy, the community's life, and service.

John Roberto offers practical and pastoral suggestions for forming the baptized faithful through a model of Church-centered faith formation that integrates liturgy, justice, and catechesis. He believes that the process of bringing people to see the relationship between the Church's liturgical life and the work of justice would be greatly enhanced by understanding catechesis as an essential element in a more comprehensive approach to faith formation.

Finally, Tom East focuses on the task of forming youth for justice and worship. He notes that for youth, the relationship between justice and liturgy is of particular importance because it is "a litmus test for relevancy." "Youth," he says," will be inspired by the active service and authentic worship they see in lives of faith in the community." In turn, youth will inspire the community with their energy, ideas, and creativity.

Two of the conference workshops engaged the participants in considering the importance of liturgical preparation and preaching in forming servants of justice. To underscore the serious and holy nature of the work of liturgical preparation, Godfrey Mullen, o.s.b., describes it as an "act of justice." "Done well," he says, "liturgical preparation itself is communion. It is proclamation. It is reconciliation." He then explores these three ways of thinking about liturgical preparation and raises important questions for those entrusted with preparing liturgies.

Finally, Del Staigers says that "preaching must lead us to believe that our faith has everything to do with our daily lives." Moreover, he argues that "all homilies should make a statement of justice." Justice requires that preaching address our relationship with God and with one another as part of the same experience. Staigers gives practical suggestions for how preachers can respond to the demands of preaching justice.

The conference closed with the presentation of the Michael Mathis Award to *Worship*, the highly regarded journal published by Saint John's Abbey, Collegeville, Minnesota. The Center for Pastoral Liturgy presents the Mathis Award each year to a person or organization that has made a significant contribution to the renewal of Catholic worship in the United States. Given the theme of the 2001 conference, honoring *Worship* with the award was particularly appropriate. Father Ostdiek said it well in his opening address: "There could be no better theme in this diamond jubilee year of *Worship* magazine. One need only glance through the early issues of what was then called *Orate Fratres* to see how thoroughly liturgy and social action were woven together and permeated its pages. That was due in no small measure to the vision and passion of Virgil Michael, O.S.B., who founded *Orate Fratres* in 1926." R. Kevin Seasoltz, O.S.B., general editor of *Worship,* responded to the award.

Admittedly, the 2001 conference could only scratch the surface of an area that is much bigger than any one gathering could address in a comprehensive manner. Yet, as I say this, the encouraging words Dom Virgil Michel wrote to Catherine de Hueck Doherty come to mind:

> Isn't that the way all things start, bit by bit? The mustard tree the Lord spoke of will grow to stature only in time and at the pleasure of the Holy Spirit and all we can do is scratch the surface and plant the little seed.

My hope is that the gathering in June of 2001 at Notre Dame planted seeds, and that in time and at the pleasure of the Holy Spirit, the seeds—like each of us, human beings made in the image and likeness of a just and loving God—will grow to full stature.

Anne Y. Koester
Notre Dame Center for Pastoral Liturgy

Abbreviations

DAL	*Apostolicam Actuositatem:* Decree on the Apostolate of the Laity, Vatican Council II (1965)
GIRM	*General Instruction on the Roman Missal,* 2nd edition, Sacred Congregation for Divine Worship, ICEL (1975)
GS	*Gaudium et Spes:* Pastoral Constitution on the Church in the Modern World, Vatican Council II (1965)
LG	*Lumen Gentium:* Dogmatic Constitution on the Church, Vatican Council II (1964)
MCW	*Music in Catholic Worship,* Bishops' Committee on the Liturgy of the United States Catholic Conference (1972)
NAB	*New American Bible with Revised New Testament,* The Confraternity of Christian Doctrine (1986)
NCCB	National Conference of Catholic Bishops
NJB	*New Jerusalem Bible,* ed. H. Wansbrough, GC (1985)
NRSV	*New Revised Standard Version of the Bible with Apocrypha* (New York: Oxford University Press, 1989)
USCC	United States Catholic Conference
SC	*Sacrosanctum Concilium:* The Constitution on the Sacred Liturgy, Vatican Council II (1963)

Gilbert Ostdiek, O.F.M.

Liturgy and Justice:
The Legacy that Awaits Us

The theme of this conference is "Liturgy and Justice: To Worship God in Spirit and Truth." There could be no better theme in this diamond jubilee year of *Worship* magazine. One need only glance through the early issues of what was then called *Orate Fratres* to see how thoroughly liturgy and social action were woven together and permeated its pages. That was due in no small measure to the vision and passion of Virgil Michel, O.S.B., who founded *Orate Fratres* in 1926. He and his successors at *Worship* and The Liturgical Press have kept before our eyes the vision of what it means to worship God in spirit and in truth. To them we owe a great debt of thanks.

My task is to reflect on the legacy of liturgy and justice that is ours to receive. Our guides for this retrospect are some of the pioneers of the American liturgical movement, who labored to integrate liturgy and social justice. What is the vision they have left us?

A Vision of Liturgy and Justice. As we think of the pioneers who have blazed the trail for us, an image in Hebrews 11 comes to mind. There, the author summons from the past a great cloud of witnesses of the community's faith, who march in glorious review before the reader's eyes. We, too, are blessed to have a great cloud of witnesses to invoke today. As we call their roll, let us listen to their words and reflect on them.[1]

The standard bearer who leads our procession of witnesses is Virgil Michel (1890–1938). He, more than anyone else who worked on these shores, captured the vision that brought liturgy and social action together. His study of social philosophy led Michel to focus on the role and mission of the laity in the Church and the contribution Catholic social thought could make to the social change needed in the early twentieth century. During a sojourn in Europe, he wedded that vision to the great new development taking place in ecclesiology and liturgy. In an early issue of *Orate Fratres* he wrote:

> Active participation in the liturgy is the means to familiarize the faithful with the mystical body doctrine. . . . He who lives the liturgy will in due time feel the mystical body idea developing in his mind and growing upon him, will come to realize that he is drinking at the very fountain of the true Christian spirit which is destined to reconstruct the Social Order.[2]

This passage weaves together the central insights that gave shape and texture to his life's work. His words can be parsed into four themes: (1) liturgy manifests and is the action of the Mystical Body; (2) active participation in the liturgy is the means by which the faithful come to understand that mystery

---

[1] For fuller accounts, see Kenneth Himes, "Eucharist and Justice: Assessing the Legacy of Virgil Michel," *Worship* 62 (1988) 201–23; Bryan Hehir, "Liturgy and Social Justice: Past Relationships and Future Possibilities," *Liturgy and Social Justice: Celebrating Rites—Proclaiming Rights,* ed. Edward Grosz (Collegeville: The Liturgical Press, 1989) 40–61; Keith Pecklers, *The Unread Vision: The Liturgical Movement in the United States of America 1926–1955* (Collegeville: The Liturgical Press, 1998); Theodore Ross, "The Synthesis of Liturgy and Justice: Five Portraits," *Living No Longer for Ourselves: Liturgy and Justice in the Nineties,* eds. Kathleen Hughes and Mark Francis (Collegeville: The Liturgical Press, 1991) 17–35. Many of the quotations that follow can also be found in Kathleen Hughes, ed., *How Firm a Foundation: Voices of the Early Liturgical Movement* (Chicago: Liturgy Training Publications, 1990).

[2] Virgil Michel, "With Our Readers," *Orate Fratres* 5 (1930–31) 431.

and make it their own; (3) liturgy thus celebrated is the fountain of the true Christian spirit; and (4) that spirit has the power to reconstruct the social order. What do the pioneers have to tell us about each of these themes?

Liturgy Manifests and Is the Action of the Mystical Body

Virgil Michel. In the preface to the first issue of *Orate Fratres*, Michel introduced his readers to the concept of the "mystic Christ." For him, this idea was the antidote to the subjectivism and individualism that plagued both Church and society. He later wrote:

> There is only one answer I know of to the problem of the balanced harmony between the individual and the social: *the mystical body of Christ*. There the individual retains his full responsibility, the fullest possibility of greater realization of the dignity as a member of Christ; yet he is ever a member of the fellowship of Christ, knit closely with his fellow members into a compact body by the indwelling Spirit of Christ. *There* is the pattern of all social life lived by the individuals.[3]

Eucharist calls us to transcend the dichotomy between individual and group—"One bread, one body . . ."

William Huelsmann. In the mid 1930s, when millions had been impoverished because of the depression and the great Midwestern drought, he wrote:

> The most terrible specter which nations are facing today is the economic problem. Its essence is the lack of realization of our interdependence in regard to our physical and moral well-being. There is, without the least doubt, no truth so wonderfully adapted to win the minds and hearts of men and women to this realization as the truth of the communion of saints, our living oneness as members in the Mystical Body of Christ, the spearhead truth of the liturgical movement.[4]

---

[3] Virgil Michel, "Natural and Supernatural Society," *Orate Fratres* 10 (1935–36) 244–45 (emphasis original).

[4] William Huelsmann, "Life in Christ," *Orate Fratres* 11 (1937) 257–58.

Interdependence, belonging to one another, to a communion of saints, is the spearhead truth the liturgy teaches us. Baptized into Christ, "we are members of one another" (Eph 4:25).[5]

Bernard Laukemper, the "patriarch" of the Liturgical Conference, in whose rectory basement it was born, once wrote: "The parish is the mystical Christ in miniature. The liturgy is the mystical Christ at worship. The Mass is the highest expression of this liturgical activity of the mystical Christ."[6] What a stunning theology of the local church! The Mystical Body is not some ethereal ideal, but rather the motley band of folks who make up the local community, summoned to prayer on Sunday and sent back into their world until they gather again. In the realms of both liturgical gathering and life of mission, the Church is as tangible as the Savior's human flesh: "What we have heard, what we have seen with our eyes, what we have looked upon and what our hands have touched" (1 John 1:1).

Martin Hellriegel said this on the eve of World War II: "Many things are rising and falling today. But there is one thing that must remain, grow and bear fruit, and that one thing is the parish, the concrete expression of the Mystical Body of Christ. . . ."[7] In a world beset, then as now, with instability and turmoil, the parish that is the local church dares to see itself as a holy temple with Christ as its cornerstone. But how can the Church become a household of faith, i.e., holds together in one house people separated by so many personal stances and loyalties, splintered by so many divisions?

Joseph Morrison. In the midst of the worldwide conflict raging in 1943, speaking on the racial problem he said: "So if we allow mere superficial differences of nation and parentage to suffocate that love for all Christ's members that is demanded of us, we injure not only ourselves but also the whole Mystical Body of Christ, and contribute to its decline. . . ."[8] Being the Body of Christ ought to bridge all differences; we are bound by

[5] Scriptural citations are taken from NAB, unless otherwise noted.
[6] Bernard Laukemper, "Points in Practice," *Orate Fratres* 12 (1938) 512.
[7] Martin Hellriegel, address at the *National Liturgical Week* (1940) 38.
[8] Joseph Morrison, "The Racial Problem," *National Liturgical Week* (1943) 113–14.

his command to love one another without distinction. "There does not exist among you Jew or Greek, slave or free, male or female. All are one in Christ Jesus" (Gal 3:28). That is what Sunday celebration is meant to tell us. To learn that, we need mystagogues like the next witness.

Cecilia Himebaugh was deeply devoted to helping people understand the connection between the liturgy and the Mystical Body. She wrote that "our task as popularizers is to make the spiritual isolationist glad to find himself in the intimate company of all his Mystical Body fellow members; to make the one who merely endures that half hour on Sunday an enthusiastic co-offerer of the Mass. . . . That's a large order, but it can be filled."[9] It is a large catechetical task indeed, and one which still must be carried out. Perhaps it begins in more modest ways than we imagine. To his severely divided community, Paul gave this simple direction: "Therefore, my brothers and sisters, when you assemble for the meal, wait for one another" (1 Cor 11:33). Wait for, wait on, attend to, serve. Such liturgical experiences of oneness are the indispensable prelude to mystagogy.

The words from all these witnesses are truly amazing. Their words were written before Pius XII had issued his encyclical on the Mystical Body. Under the inspiration of Virgil Michel and others, these pioneers had already learned about this great Pauline theme from biblical scholars, and they immediately recognized its implications for celebration of the liturgy. Foremost among those was the need for active participation by the laity.

Active Participation in Liturgy Is the Means to Understand that Mystery and Make It One's Own

Virgil Michel said, "Through the liturgy rightly understood and lived, all our life is centered in Christ and the Christ-life radiates out into every action of the day." He added:

---

[9] Cecilia Himebaugh, "Popularizing the Liturgy," *Orate Fratres* 17 (1942–43) 511.

> Participation in the liturgy naturally produces in us the con-
> sciousness of our union with Christ and of our dignity as shar-
> ers in the divine nature. It brings us into contact with the
> many-sided aspects of the life of Christ, with the rich inex-
> haustible content of His life, and thus manifests the rich possi-
> bilities of our life in Him. It elevates our minds above the things
> of this earth and of self, broadens our spiritual outlook while
> deepening it, gives us . . . a better sense of unity with a sympa-
> thy for our fellow members of the body of Christ, a human fam-
> ily feeling for all mankind. . . ."[10]

It is above all in the liturgy, celebrated week after week, that
his later-day disciples get to know Christ. His way is set before
them as their way of life, set before them in sacred story, in
holy bread and cup.

Catherine de Hueck Doherty, pioneer of the lay apostolate in
Canada, said:

> The daily sacrifice, fully participated in, will open to us the
> mind of Christ, and we will radiate him in our lives. And then
> we shall be able to go forth and fight the good fight of Christ
> against poverty, misery, injustice. Participation in the Mass will
> teach us the full understanding of the Mystical Body of Christ,
> leading us to a Christian sociology, which is the cornerstone of
> the Christian social order and which alone can save our mad
> world from destruction.[11]

To radiate Christ in our lives. That is what participation in the
liturgy forms us to do. There is one condition: "Make your own
the mind of Christ Jesus" (NJB Phil 2:5). How else can we radiate Christ?

Hans Ansgar Reinhold left Germany during Hitler's climb to
power and became a vigorous protestor against anti-Semitism
and every social injustice. He said:

---

[10] Virgil Michel, *The Liturgy of the Church: According to the Roman Rite*
(New York: Macmillan, 1937) 60–61.

[11] Catherine de Hueck Doherty, "I Saw Christ Today," *Orate Fratres* 12
(1938) 309–10.

> There is a coherence between life outside and within us, Christ and the world, our mind and the economy of salvation, our person and the Church. When we begin to see this, to experience the truth and the fact, we then are consciously living members of the living Christ, the Church. Then we realize that the sacraments and the liturgy are functions of Christ who becomes mysteriously contemporaneous to us, veiled and disguised under appallingly plain symbols—bread, wine, water, oil, words and actions, fellow-men. When all this invades our consciousness, then we begin to understand and we *become* liturgical.[12]

That is the moment when our liturgy becomes truly authentic, for then we understand what it is to be living members of Christ and, with him, to worship God everywhere, "in spirit and in truth" (John 4:23-24). For "[it] is through him that we address our Amen to God when we worship together" (2 Cor 1:20).

Godfrey Diekmann was Michel's successor as editor of *Orate Fratres/Worship* for twenty-five years, a mainstay of the Liturgical Conference, a marcher at Selma. He wrote, "The eucharist is not something static. The gift becomes the obligation; the eucharist is something dynamic, a life that demands to be lived. We receive Christ . . . not to keep him for ourselves but to give him to others so that they may recognize him in us."[13] Eucharist demands that we learn from him to become, like him, "bread for the life of the world" (John 6:51). This is not simply a matter of external conformity to Christ but of sharing in his life deep within. A theme increasingly dear to Diekmann is what the writers of the Eastern Church call our divinization. In Christ we are truly God's children by adoption.

Active participation, in the minds of these pioneers, has little to do with external busyness. It has everything to do with what Mary Collins has called "contemplative participation,"[14] seeing

[12] Hans Ansgar Reinhold, "More or Less Liturgical," *Orate Fratres* 13 (1939) 154–55 (emphasis original).

[13] Godfrey Diekmann, "The Theology of Worship," *Theology Digest* 10 (1962) 140–41.

[14] Mary Collins, *Contemplative Participation: Sacrosanctum Concilium Twenty-Five Years Later* (Collegeville: The Liturgical Press, 1990) 75–86.

with the heart into the mystery within, Christ present and acting among us still.

Liturgy Thus Celebrated Is the Fountain of the True Christian Spirit

Virgil Michel was very taken with the words of Pius X, which were later enshrined in the Constitution on the Sacred Liturgy 14: "The primary and indispensable source of the Christian spirit is the active participation in the most holy mysteries and in the public and solemn prayer of the church." Michel described his vision and yearning for what participation can achieve:

> There [in the Mass] every action of our lives must be centered and thence it must derive its inspiration. If we can learn again to offer our whole selves consciously on the altar of Christ's own sacrifice, our body and our soul, our actions and all the material possessions we have; if we can realize better that this offering is made in union with all our brothers and sisters and is made by each for all and by all for each; and if we can learn to grasp by growing degrees the more sublime truth that this offering of ours is merged with the very sacrifice of Christ himself—then, indeed, shall we be better able to assign to material goods their rightful place in human life. . . .[15]

To offer our whole selves consciously, to merge this offering with that of Christ himself. This is the heart of it all and the fountain from which to draw the true Christian spirit.

Reynold Hillenbrand loved to share the vision of liturgy and life. Writing at the end of the great drought of the 1930s and on the eve of World War II, he found a silver lining even then:

> We might not be as far as we are except for the last sobering decade—with its disillusionment; with its struggle, its suffering; with its revelation of hard realities, too easily overlooked; with its mounting feeling of the necessity of reconstructing this

[15] Virgil Michel, "Modern Greed and the Mass," *Orate Fratres* 11 (1937) 323–24.

poor, sorry world—of the necessity of a profound renewal of the Christian spirit...[16]

No timid vision. That spirit cannot be confined within the walls of a church or the time it takes to celebrate liturgy. Liturgy and life flow into each other. One who has been imbibed with the true spirit of the Lord in the liturgy comes to understand that all life, like his, is "a living sacrifice of praise" (Eucharistic Prayer IV; see Rom 12:1). And that must be shared.

Dorothy Day was cofounder of *The Catholic Worker* and the Catholic Worker Movement. Spreading the doctrine of the Mystical Body was her passion:

> [T]o be in church isn't to be calmed down, as some people say they get when they are at Mass. I'm worked up. I'm excited by being so close to Jesus, but the closer I get, the more I worry about what He wants of us, what He would have us do before we die.[17]

What would Jesus have us do to spread his spirit? May we always feel that same excitement and enthusiasm to help the Christian spirit spill over into the lives of others!

William Leonard taught liturgy and founded a school of social work. He wrote:

> It would be a poor liturgical life, however, that would be somehow suspended as we went out of the church, not to be resumed until we entered again. Everything we have seen and heard and done in our worship of God should have had its formative influence on us. We should go out from our community prayer new men, determined once more to publish Christ by our manner of living.[18]

To publish Christ by our manner of living—what a lovely way to name what liturgy can inspire!

---

[16] Reynold Hillenbrand, address at the *National Liturgical Week* (1940) 5.

[17] Robert Coles, *Dorothy Day: A Radical Devotion* (Reading, Mass.: Addison-Wesley, 1987) 76–77.

[18] William Leonard, *New Horizons in Catholic Worship* (Wichita, Kans.: The Liturgical Commission, 1964) 62.

Clearly, for these pioneers, liturgy and life are one, seamlessly woven together by the spirit Christians learn from Christ. The Amen spoken so readily and often in liturgy is not just an empty ritual exchange; it is a commitment to be carried out in life as well.

The Christian Spirit Has the Power to Reconstruct the Social Order

Virgil Michel. We turn once more to Virgil Michel, who saw social regeneration as the capstone to complete his vision. Listen to his simple, compelling syllogism: "Pius X tells us that the liturgy is the indispensable source of the true Christian spirit; Pius XI says that the true Christian spirit is indispensable for social regeneration. Hence the conclusion: The liturgy is the indispensable basis of Christian social regeneration."[19] These words are so compelling that no further argument is needed, only willing hands to carry them out. "Blessed are they who hear the word of God and keep it" (Luke 11:28).

Daniel Cantwell, who was actively involved in many social causes, said this: "Indeed we might seriously consider whether . . . it is possible to restore all things in Christ on Sunday until we first show ourselves equally concerned with the necessity of restoring to the working lives of the multitudes their Christian dignity and human rights."[20] Restoring all things in Christ is indeed a tall order. Sunday alone will not suffice; what is called for is concrete action that seeks to affirm and restore the dignity and rights of others. "Let us love, not in word or speech, but in truth and action" (NRSV 1 John 3:18).

Hans Ansgar Reinhold, whom we have already met, also said that "since we are members of that Mystical Body, which prolongs the incarnation, the state of the body social is a liturgical concern . . . we who claim to live by [the sacraments] must be found in the forefront of those who work for a new society

[19] Virgil Michel, "Liturgy as the Basis of Social Regeneration," *Orate Fratres* 9 (1934–35) 545.
[20] Daniel Cantwell, "What Has Happened to Sunday?" *National Liturgical Week* (1949) 33.

built according to the justice and charity of Christ." He went on to call those interested in liturgical renewal to become actively involved in charitable efforts, in employers' councils and housing committees, in interracial groups, in campaigning for medical services for those unable to afford them, to "make the cause of enslaved nations a matter of their own heart."[21] Let there be no divided hearts, no split in our lives between Mystical Body and social body, between life of prayer and life in a world too often bereft of justice and charity. "How does the love of God abide in anyone who has the world's goods and sees a brother or sister in need and yet refuses help?" (NRSV 1 John 3:17).

Mary Perkins Ryan, whose vision interwove the catechetical and liturgical movements, said:

> A person interested in the liturgy . . . must have no fragmentary interest in the concerns of the church. They are all rooted in the liturgy. It is infinitely sad when someone devoted to the liturgy will minimize an interest in the social doctrine, in rural life, in the racial problems, in international life, in Catholic action. We cannot, of course, have a comprehensive knowledge of all these things, but we must have an interest and a sympathy. When you find a person who is lacking in that interest and sympathy, you have found a person who is imperfectly schooled in the liturgy, who does not understand it in its completeness, who does not have the vision it is able to give.[22]

No fragmentary interest. What is needed is thorough schooling, through catechesis and celebration, in the vision liturgy is able to instill.

And so the last of our cloud of pioneer witnesses has passed in review. But like the account in Hebrews, there is yet one more pioneer who must hold our gaze even after the others have passed from sight. After invoking the great heroes of the past, the author of Hebrews concludes: "Therefore, since we

---

[21] Hans Ansgar Reinhold, "Social Leaven," *Orate Fratres* 25 (1951–52) 518, 519.

[22] Mary Perkins Ryan, *The Sacramental Way* (Kansas City, Mo.: Sheed and Ward, 1948) 38–39.

for our part are surrounded by this cloud of witnesses, let us lay aside every encumbrance of sin which clings to us and persevere in running the race which lies ahead; let us keep our eyes fixed on Jesus, who inspires and perfects our faith" (Heb 12:1-2). Let us keep our eyes fixed on Jesus. He is the "Just One," Scriptures tell us (Acts 3:14). It is his memory we keep in liturgy, his work that is enacted, his Amen that we voice again and again and carry with us into the world.

A Legacy that Awaits Us

Such, then, is the legacy that awaits us. What does it mean for us?

A legacy for our times. The pioneers' legacy is not a treasure to be hoarded unchanged, but a way of acting, of visioning for the future. They inherited a past in which they gloried; they also read the signs of the times and let the past inspire them to do what had to be done in their day. Michel put it this way: "We are living in our own age, and while the past can indicate to us the spirit of the liturgy more clearly, it can not decide for us all our present applications of that spirit, the total manner in which that spirit must manifest itself today."[23] We honor the pioneers best by following their example.

A half-century and more has passed, but many of the ecclesial and societal issues they faced remain with us. Individualism and subjectivism are still hallmarks of our culture. Poverty persists even in the midst of our plenty; the gap between rich and poor people and nations widens. We have lived through wars, a holocaust, and genocide on a scale few would have imagined then. Racial and other hatreds stubbornly persist despite consciousness-raising movements. Life is taken casually with little thought or remorse. To compound these ills, we often feel powerless in the face of unresponsive political systems, the complexities of a global economy, and the rapid pace of relentless change. That powerlessness too easily provokes us to anger and rage against others.

[23] Virgil Michel, "The Meaning of the Church's Liturgy," *America* 34 (April 3, 1926) 587.

The Church in the U.S. has not escaped all this. Since the pioneers first broached their vision, the Church has entered mainstream America. The culture's ills have too readily become our ills as Church. Incivility and even demonizing others are contagions that we have caught from society. This is a major pastoral problem, indeed a scandal, if we take seriously the Lord's final command to love and serve one another as he did.

What the pioneers hold up before our eyes is a vision that takes belief in the Mystical Body with utmost seriousness. The true Christian spirit welling up in liturgy teaches us to work for the solidarity of and accept the members not only of that body, but also of the entire human family. Belief in the Mystical Body tells us we belong to each other and are responsible for each other. That is the heart of their legacy.

Liturgy's humble role. Were these pioneers naïve and unrealistic in dreaming that full participation in the liturgy would have that impact? After all, we have enjoyed that participation for more than three decades now, and their vision remains a distant goal. What might need adjusting is any expectation we harbor that a fully participative liturgy can accomplish the dream of ecclesial and social solidarity all by itself. Liturgy does have a part to play, but it cannot bear that weight alone. Nathan Mitchell said it well:

> Liturgy is neither the problem nor the solution. *Liturgiam authenticam, Built of Living Stones,* the revised GIRM 2000—none of these things deserve the time and attention we give them. Liturgy is a humble, earthly means to an end, and the end is people—hungry people, homeless people, victims of violence, war, and oppression, children sold as slave labor, lives destroyed by disease and famine. And yes, the affluent American suburbanites as well. All these are the "end" for whom liturgy is a means. . . . These are the things that matter; these are the "issues" that need our energy and our insight.[24]

---

[24] Nathan Mitchell, "Liturgy in the United States: The State of the Question," a talk delivered at "Differing Visions, One Communion," a conference sponsored by The Liturgical Press, Collegeville, Minnesota, June 7–10, 2001.

And so the question confronting us is this: Have we liturgists focused too narrowly on the liturgy, on getting it right and getting it done? The Vatican II renewal has surely entailed massive pastoral effect. The work is relentless, and too often liturgy occasions contention and division. There is wisdom for us in Mitchell's words. Liturgy is neither the problem nor the solution; its role is humble. If the liturgy manifests the mystery of the Church (SC 2), tensions and divisions at work in the Church will manifest themselves when we gather to pray. What our times seem to demand, then, is that we place pastoral priority on building a more caring and loving community, and that we find a larger vision of pastoral ministry which can help us reconnect the dots between all the various ministries, especially liturgy and justice.

Liturgy woven into the fabric of ministry. If liturgy cannot do it alone, what other forms of ministry need to accompany it? This is really the larger question of how to shape, or reshape, ministry for the future. The Emmaus story (Luke 24:13-35) offers us a model to ponder.[25] The journey of the two disciples moves from disillusionment to full Easter faith, which dawned in their hearts when their eyes were opened. The Stranger who walks with them on the way ministers to them according to their need of the moment. In contemporary terms, those moments of ministry can be named as pastoral care, word, sacrament, mystagogy, and mission. The outcome of the story depends on each of those moments.

Several lessons for ministry can be drawn from the Emmaus account. First, ministry has less to do with the specific tasks we perform than with disciples on a faith journey. The high demands of preparing and celebrating good liturgies may subtly lead us to focus on tasks rather than on people. There is so much to attend to and do. Second, no single work of ministry, even the liturgy, can by itself bring disciples to their journey's end. Each depends on the success of others. In each of these ministries the demands are now great. More ministers are

[25] See Gilbert Ostdiek, "Response to the Mathis Award," *The Many Presences of Christ,* eds. Timothy Fitzgerald and David Lysik (Chicago: Liturgy Training Publications, 1999) 9–11.

needed, and more stress is rightly being placed on proper preparation and formation, a kind of ministerial specialization and professionalization. But this has too readily led us to compartmentalize various ministries. Do we even talk to one another about them? What the Emmaus paradigm urges is that we find ways to re-weave the ministries. Third, in this model two things bind the ministries together and demand more continuity. One is that disciples make the journey. We ought never forget that people and their journey come first. The other is the Stranger who is companion and minister to them on the way. We need to learn again that ministry, of whatever sort, is not a noun but a verb. We each act in the name of the Lord Jesus, as the Stranger's guise he wears to meet and serve his wayfaring disciples in their moments of need.[26]

The pioneers did just such a weaving of ministries in their own day. They constantly integrated pastoral concerns, catechesis about the Mystical Body, celebration of the liturgy, and the search for justice. They would never have conceived of parceling out liturgy and justice to different sets of folks; they were each committed to both.

Liturgy rehearses justice. The fourth and final challenge raised for us by the pioneers is that of wedding liturgy and justice. Too often liturgy and justice ministries go their separate ways. Liturgists may pick justice as a theme for a celebration, or social justice activities may attend liturgy for spiritual support, but the connection is not intrinsic and each of these ministries could be carried on just as well without the other.[27]

The better approach for liturgists to take is to see just action as something that must be deeply embedded in the liturgy itself; it is not an optional add-on. An image used by Mark Searle says it well:

---

[26] *Catechism of the Catholic Church* 427 makes this point in regard to catechists.

[27] For further commentary, see John Egan, "Liturgy and Justice: An Unfinished Agenda," *Origins* 13 (1983) 245, 247–53; Kathleen Hughes, "Liturgy and Justice: An Intrinsic Relationship," *Living No Longer for Ourselves,* 36–52.

The liturgical assembly, then, is the place where justice is proclaimed, but it is neither a classroom nor a political rally nor a
hearing. It is more like a rehearsal room where actions must be
repeated over and over until they are thoroughly assimilated
and perfected—until, that is, the actors have totally identified
with the part assigned to them.[28]

Our very way of celebrating liturgy must rehearse justice.
Now that full participation is the order of the day, it is perhaps
time to examine our conscience. Are our celebrations making
us more just? Do they rehearse justice or injustice?[29] *Sacrosanctum Concilium* 14 says that full participation of the faithful is
their right and duty by reason of baptism. GIRM 313 directs
that priests planning liturgy should put consideration of the
religious needs and spiritual good of the assembly before their
personal outlook. Thus, a celebration that excludes full participation of people or disregards due adaptation to their spiritual
needs is itself an act of injustice. Such a celebration cannot help
but school us wordlessly in the practice of injustice, even as we
say we keep the memory of the Just One. Conversely, a liturgy
that is celebrated as justly as we possibly can will rehearse us
in God's ways of justice and compassion for all.

The pioneers dreamed no small dreams. Liturgy actively
celebrated by the members of Christ's Body would surely open
up that mystery; it would model and bring about a radically
transformed Church and society. We may not dare to dream
that large, for we have learned through hard experience that
even with full participation the liturgy is not a panacea for the
world's ill, or even the Church's. But the renewed liturgy has
made a difference in people's lives, calling them into community, deepening their prayer, and creating new spiritual
hungers. So we are not without hope for what the liturgy can
accomplish. If we attend to the people who celebrate and to the

[28] Mark Searle, "Serving the Lord with Justice," *Liturgy and Social Justice,*
ed. Mark Searle (Collegeville: The Liturgical Press, 1980) 32.

[29] See my "Liturgical Catechesis and Justice," *Living No Longer for Ourselves,* 170–84; and "Liturgy as Catechesis for Life," *Liturgical Ministry* 7
(Spring 1998) 81–82.

things of the spirit that matter to them—walking with them in their daily struggle to live good lives, helping them find their story in the Christ-story, feeding their spiritual hungers, helping them treat one another with a little more love and compassion for the love of Christ—who would dare say that the pioneers' dreams are out of reach?

The vision they have left us is breathtaking, a legacy well worth receiving with awe and respect for what they set out to accomplish in their day. It is not something already completed; rather, it is a task given over to us to carry out again in our day. It is a legacy whose doing awaits us. And surely there is much to be done, in ways both great and small, to reweave liturgy and justice, and indeed all the ministries, once more into a seamless whole. The legacy that awaits us is to recreate and fashion their legacy anew and to bequeath it in turn to those who follow us.

Rehearsing the Reign of God
by Building Just Communities

About Focus: HOPE

Mrs. Josaitis is the cofounder and executive director of Focus: HOPE, a civil and human rights organization located in Detroit. Josaitis and the late Father William T. Cunningham (1930–97) started Focus: HOPE in 1968 in response to the city's devastating 1967 riots. What was first a grassroots movement has now grown to over seven hundred colleagues supported by fifty-one thousand volunteers. Focus: HOPE is recognized worldwide for the solutions it has found to the problems of racism, poverty, and injustice. Its career training and education programs, the Centers of Opportunity, have helped thousands access the economic mainstream. Its Commodity Supplemental Food Program provides food to forty-three thousand seniors, mothers, and children every month. In addition, the organization offers Montessori-based childcare, business conference facilities, community arts projects, and other outreach services.

I want to take you on a journey, a journey of intelligent, practical action to overcome racism, poverty, and injustice. The journey began in the 1960s with a Catholic priest, Father William Cunningham, who was an English professor at Sacred Heart Seminary in Detroit, a weekend pastor at a suburban parish, and a very gifted speaker. I was a suburban housewife, raising

19

five children and living a very comfortable life. Father Cunningham was the weekend pastor at our parish. My husband and I attended the Masses at which Father Cunningham presided, because he could always take the Gospel, give the history of it, and translate it for today. He also gave people a challenge —something to take with them as they walked out of the church doors. My husband and I became very good friends with Father Cunningham.

However, on this journey, the most significant emotional event happened one night when I was watching television. I was watching the Nuremberg trials, and I was appalled at what I was seeing. Suddenly, that program was interrupted by the news of the civil rights march in Mississippi. I sat there and watched as policemen rode through the group of marchers, giving the marchers electric shocks with cattle prodders or turning fire hoses on them. I watched as the police flipped children, seniors, and marchers in the air, and turned dogs loose on the crowd. I cried, asking myself, "What would I have done if I had lived in Germany during the Nuremberg trials? Would I have pretended that I hadn't seen anything? Would I have become involved? What would I have done? And what am I doing about what is going on in my country today?" The experience changed me instantly.

I became a very strong supporter of Dr. Martin Luther King Jr. as did Father Cunningham who marched with Dr. King in Selma, Alabama. Father Cunningham and I talked extensively about civil rights. When the Detroit riots hit in 1967, the immediate question was, "What are we going to do?" Father Cunningham left his teaching career and took a parish, Madonna parish, which was in the heart of the city of Detroit. My husband and I sold our home and moved into an integrated neighborhood that was also in the heart of the city. When we did this, my mother hired an attorney to try and take my five children away from me; my father-in-law disowned us; and my brother-in-law asked me to use my maiden name so I wouldn't embarrass the family. My family reacted in this way not because they didn't love me but because they thought I had completely flipped. They could not understand my actions. My mother eventually changed and became a very strong supporter, and my brother-in-law now thinks I am cool. But it was a challenging period.

Father Cunningham was a visionary and an extremely articulate communicator. He and I wrote a mission statement for Focus: HOPE on March 8, 1968, which reads:

> Recognizing the dignity and beauty of every person, we pledge intelligent and practical action to overcome racism, poverty and injustice. And to build a metropolitan community where all people may live in freedom, harmony, trust and affection. Black and white, yellow, brown and red from Detroit and its suburbs of every economic status, national origin and religious persuasion we join in this covenant.

This statement is what Focus: HOPE is all about. And with everything we do, we ask, "Is it intelligent? Is it practical? Is it going to reach our goals?"

Father Cunningham passed away four years ago, after battling cancer for a year. During his illness, he only asked one thing of me: "Eleanor, do not put my name on a boulevard and do not name a building after me. Just make my work live on, make my work live on."

[Further information about Focus: HOPE may be found by visiting the organization's web site: <www.focushope.edu>.]

Rehearsing the Reign of God
by Building Just Communities

New Community Corporation (NCC) is a community development corporation (CDC). As a CDC, it focuses on low-income
neighborhood development, employs a comprehensive strategy,
and seeks the priorities of the community. It never imposes a
top-down plan, and it always stresses self-sufficiency. NCC
was founded in Newark, New Jersey, one of the poorest cities
in America, and was born from the civil rights movement in an
African American Catholic parish. Although many would call
it a faith-based initiative, NCC is now independent of formal
church affiliation. Still, the role of religion is very powerful; it is
ecumenical.

Today NCC employs over twenty-three hundred people who
work in its various operations, touching about fifty thousand
lives each day. Its components include three thousand units of
housing which are self-managed, maintained, and secured. Se-
curity operations alone employs 154 men and women. Health
care services include a 180-bed nursing home, Home Health
Care, Home Friends Chore Service, four medical day care
centers, and a visiting nurse service. A total of 950 persons staff
this almost totally Medicare/Medicaid supported system for
our elderly population.

Educational components include two parochial schools, two
charter schools, and one traditional public school (which, because 84 percent of its student body reside in NCC housing,

operates more as a community school). Acting as real estate de-
veloper, NCC helped to create a third charter school and with
a community day care provider, offers eight hundred early
childhood slots in seven centers. A new NCC day care center
provides another two hundred openings.

Our Workforce Development Center is a state-of-the-art facil-
ity that annually trains over five hundred individuals, many of
whom are former welfare recipients, in twelve different skill
areas. The Youth Automotive Training Center is a partnership
with Ford Motor Company to prepare often at-risk young people
for careers as auto technicians in a field which falls short by
sixty thousand workers annually. The program is a national
Ford prototype.

NCC's Human Development Department is the lead agency
in welfare to work, since we feel that to assist very low-income
people to greater financial independence is part of our mission.
In addition, the department runs numerous youth programs.

NCC has twelve for-profit corporations. Among these are a
major food supermarket, a restaurant, a fashion center, and a
housing manufacturing plant. The plant is an eighty-thousand-
square-foot factory that makes housing components, panels, and
trusses. These businesses provide needed jobs and strengthen
the vitality of the parent, NCC.

Community banking is important to our mission. The NCC
Federal Credit Union provides an under-served community
with banking services. It offers opportunities for financial education, home mortgages, individual development accounts,
micro-loans, and traditional loans. The Business Development
Fund, working with eight banks, provides capital for new and
small businesses to create new jobs. Garden State Affordable
Housing was created so NCC could help small community-
based organizations and organizations addressing special
needs to secure investment for their housing through the
federal low-income housing tax credit program.

Finally, many religious communities are part of our social
investment fund, making economic development possible.
However, it would be nice if institutions of higher learning
would join their parent religious communities in this program
of social investment.

Newark, New Jersey, does not always enjoy the most favorable media coverage. We at NCC attempt to cancel the negative news about our community by telling the good news, the goals and accomplishments of struggling people, through our monthly newspaper, the *Clarion*, with its circulation of forty-two thousand, and our website, <www.newcommunity.org/>.

In order to infuse the lives of our people with beauty, NCC maintains a community arts staff to promote the arts in our community. We celebrate our diversity by sharing the native cultures of our many employees and residents who have come here from Africa, the West Indies, and Latin America. We promote jazz with its roots deep in the American culture, especially as representing the African American contribution. Our properties exhibit outdoor sculptures, and public art exhibits are part of our regular experience.

The Hispanic Development Corporation was founded to ensure that the Hispanic community felt most welcome at NCC. It provides programs specifically designed for the Hispanic community, and it connects Hispanics with existing NCC programs.

In the last seven years, an increasing amount of NCC efforts have been devoted to international groups. In the last three years, visitors from over twenty-five countries have visited us each year for exposure to community development. NCC has become involved in the peace process in Northern Ireland and sponsors a demonstration farm in Kenya. It is all part of being world citizens.

What has taken place was not an easy journey, nor did it happen all at once. To go back to the beginning, to the very roots of the NCC story, we must return to July of 1967, when civil unrest came to a sudden crescendo with a violent community uprising. It led to twenty-six deaths in four days. Among the dead was a mother of three killed in her own apartment, a child shot dead on the street, and a fire captain whose line of duty exposed him to rifle fire. The response from those in power, including the archbishop at the time, was that communist organizers caused the civil disorders. The governor established a board of inquiry to address the real issues and recommend a response.

An African American parish located about one and one half blocks from the site of the beginning of the civil disorders did respond. With no support from the archdiocese and despite its opposition, New Community was born. It did receive support from many suburban Catholic parishes along with suburban Protestant churches and synagogues.

The parish took a firm stand, making it clear that the Church must make a positive response to the cries of the people. This position was based not on financial resources of the Church but on faith that God did not want racism, urban bias, and moral judgment of the poor to justify a negative response. The parish believed that God's love is universal and that our trust in God's love would give to a small community of faith all that it needed to bring about positive change. Nine people, some of the parish and some not of the parish, agreed to a twenty-year commitment to a board called the New Community Corporation. Thus began a journey of faith.

The eucharistic community of Queen of Angels parish was the base community, but since both Catholics and non-Catholics would be involved, the organization sought to root itself in a more ecumenical function for religion, much like the role of religion in the civil rights movement. Religion gave the movement the principles, the sense of Divine Power, and ritual. Catholic social teaching gave the group road signs, which made the way clear even in the most difficult days. As Catholics we shared the same vision and faith with others not of our faith, but we did not share the Eucharist. This has always made the journey both sad and happy. While it was special to share with them as people of faith, it was difficult not to share at the Table of the Lord. The building of God's kingdom here is but a glimpse of God's love for us, which reaches into every aspect of people's lives. Yet, the final kingdom is described as a banquet to be shared by all, with the present banquet as a foretaste of what is to come.

On my recent visit to Kenya, the power of the eucharistic banquet could not have been more intense in showing faith in God and the universality of the message of hope than at the parish of Our Lady of Guadeloupe. There, over one thousand persons from a squatter community within the city of Nairobi attended the Eucharist, which is celebrated in Swahili. In that city over sixty percent, or 1.8 million people, live in slums without water, a sewage system, garbage removal, police, roads, or any of the physical infrastructure that we take for granted in a modern city. Yet, the faith of these people is celebrated four times each Sunday at the central church and at three outstations. Material deprivation does not dampen the attractiveness of Jesus' message of hope and unity. The message is not only for the future but also for the present. Liturgy renewed the spirit of the people, and they went forth to face another week. Their quest had a deep spiritual experience within them.

On October 22, 2000, Father Tom Peterson, O.P., chancellor of Seton Hall University, died. He was much loved, not only by the Seton Hall community, but by people of color in Newark, for among his many deeds of kindness Father Peterson taught an open enrollment, free-tuition credit course in the Central Ward of Newark, a community of African Americans. He taught the course for six years as his personal commitment to the community in order to encourage those who lacked the confidence either to start college or to return to college after they experienced what should have been a temporary setback. Each year the experience was the same: about fifteen students going to class with Father Peterson for two hours each week for fifteen weeks. Many of his students either began or returned to pursue a college degree. It was no wonder that Father Peterson's kindness was responded to with love.

When he died, call after call came to St. Rose of Lima Rectory and to the office of New Community to inquire when the funeral would take place. As he was a Dominican, the funeral was held at Providence College, where Father Peterson had been president for ten years. Seton Hall University held a memorial Mass in the auditorium because of the number of people who wanted to attend. The hall was full. Before the Mass a formal announcement was read, disinviting those who were not Catholic from receiving Communion. With that introduction, the Liturgy of the Eucharist began. Many who were not Catholic were deeply hurt. Father Peterson was also their priest; they loved him.

Earlier in the month, a funeral was held in a Catholic church in a wealthy suburb. Because it was the Mass of the Resurrection for the mother of a fellow worker, a number of employees of New Community attended, most of whom were Catholic. The same announcement about Communion was made. A number of the African-American Catholics were angry and deeply hurt because they felt the announcement was made based on the assumption that none of the African Americans in the assembly could be Catholic. They, along with the African Americans who were present and who were not Catholic, interpreted the announcement as racist. I have no way of knowing what this priest's intentions were, but I do know how our African American Catholics felt. I also know that the American Church has been a source of embarrassment to me over the issue of race during my thirty-eight years of ministry.

When we celebrate the Eucharist, although we rejoice over who is present, we should also be saddened by who is missing. African Americans are not present in significant numbers in Catholic churches, and the reason why should be obvious. It is the historical racism within the American Catholic Church. The Church will never be accused of overcompensation for the past sins of racism; for one has only to look at the present level of commitment to African Americans by the Church. It is clear that little has changed. Within my first year after ordination, I was told that there was little need to place African Americans in leadership positions in the Church for they represented such a small percentage of total Catholic population. Possibly they represent so small a percentage of the Church because so few are represented in leadership positions. The time has come for the American Church to discuss spiritual reparation to our African American brothers and sisters.

I always enjoy being part of the eucharistic celebration in other countries. It gives me a deep sense of the universal Church. My greatest experience of Church in another country was certainly my experience in Kenya, as well as the experience I had in Cuarnavaca, Mexico, with Bishop Sergio, who was a special human being. Twice a week I concelebrated with the bishop during my summer there, one day at a cloistered convent and another day at the cathedral. I cannot emphasize enough how special he was. On Sunday with the assistance of a mariachi band, he celebrated the Eucharist. After Mass he sat in the courtyard, as long lines of Mexicans from the surrounding hills came to have their children blessed. On Monday he celebrated Mass at the cloistered convent, where he preached so long that I was late for class. He was significant enough that several attempts were made on his life. Once, my parish hosted a Central American bishop as a guest for a week. He eagerly expressed his opinion that Bishop Sergio was a communist; however, I knew that Bishop Sergio loved people as Jesus loved people.

What happens to the indigenous people of Mexico and the people of the shanty cities that make up Nairobi is important to the liturgy. In liturgy, we celebrate our solidarity. The unity of all humanity, the universal call to salvation, the celebration of the Eucharist can never be celebrated unless we see ourselves as part of the human family, called to resurrection by and through Christ Jesus. Thus, the celebration of world vision should be a constant part of our liturgy and not something relegated to two homilies a year relating to Catholic missions. The word "catholic" needs to be a constant in the liturgy. The less the diversity of the parish family, the more the global view of our faith must play a major role in the liturgy.

The urban bias that has been so much part of the American scene since 1945 has had its impact on the Catholic Church. There needs to be a greater commitment to our urban parishes, along with the understanding that in the history of the Catholic Church in America, ethnic parishes played a significant role in the lives of new immigrants. Such parishes were warm homes where many of us, our forefathers and our foremothers, found our education in a sympathetic environment, where we met others who shared our faith, and where we created our own institutions. Indeed, the parish of 1860 may well have had an elementary school, a high school, and even orphanages and hospitals. Today, many descendants of the immigrants who were part of these parishes have achieved wealth and become captains of industry.

There is no reason suburban parishes cannot help support city parishes in need, so that they can respond to the many new arrivals in our cities and allow the newcomers to have their own parishes. Years ago, St. Rose of Lima parish in Newark, where I share ministry, sent large sums of money to people in what was then rural New Jersey, to enable them to buy land and build churches where wealthy suburban churches now stand. It was the vision of these urban parishes that made possible many suburban parishes.

Today many Americans, including Catholics, would prefer not to acknowledge the poor in our midst. If we do acknowledge that they exist, we take great comfort in blaming them for their plight. Thank God that God is more understanding and loving than we are.

One of the projects of interest to me was the establishment of a program on Community Development at the Catholic University of Eastern Africa. Two of the faculty members spent a month with NCC during April 2000. In May 2001, I visited Kenya with part of the purpose of my visit being the start of this program. I actually taught the first fifteen hours, which is not much when one considers the program is two months. What surprised me was what seemed to be the little involvement in the university by Catholic higher education institutions in the U.S. The university serves eight countries and would be extremely important to evangelization in this part of the world. Involvement by Catholic colleges in America would be one way to have a worldview. Further, why couldn't students in the U.S. who are buying books have the opportunity to check off another $20.00 as their donation to Catholic education in third-world countries? These could be two activities among others to teach a world vision.

In the suburban parishes, it is essential that both the liturgy and parish programs promote suburban-urban links, ethnic and racial diversity, and attitudes toward the poor that reflect the actions of Jesus. Our Christian communities must reflect the universal call to salvation by Jesus. It is also vital that the concept of a universal church with people of every physical type and ethnic group—urban, suburban, rural, and from every place in our world—be part of our liturgy. It is also essential that parish activities reflect this image of the Church so that parish liturgy and parish action are one.

Walter J. Burghardt, s.j.

Worship and Justice Reunited

Worship and justice reunited. To do justice to this challenging title, I must attempt an adventure in three areas: history, Scripture, and theology—in that order, with an effort at a swift synthesis to end it all.

I. First, a segment of liturgical history.[1] Swift indeed, only some of the more notable moments, names, and institutions, but indispensable if we are to understand how we came to where we are. Reach back to the European roots of the liturgical movement between 1833 and 1925. Following the French Revolution and the disarray of the Church, Prosper Guéranger reestablished the Benedictine abbey of Solesmes, centering monastic life on the liturgical year. His passion for a Christian life with liturgy as its source was so influential that a strong critic, Louis Bouyer, was convinced that there is no achievement in the contemporary liturgical movement that did not originate in some way with Guéranger.

There was the German liturgical movement, with its origins in the Benedictine monastery of Beuron, promoting a harmonious relationship between art and liturgy. There was Beuron's

---

[1] Here I am dependent on the splendid treatment by Keith F. Pecklers, *The Unread Vision: The Liturgical Movement in the United States of America: 1926–55* (Collegeville: The Liturgical Press, 1998), especially 1–149.

daughter house Maria Laach, with Herwegen, Mohlberg, and Casel. Casel viewed the Church as the Mystical Body of Christ, expressing itself relationally and symbolically through sacramental participation. This was one of the founding principles of the liturgical movement in the United States.

In Belgium there was the monastic community of Mont César, where the pastoral liturgical movement grew through the prophetic vision and leadership of Dom Lambert Beauduin. Beauduin was convinced that the liturgy alone could provide the grounding necessary for Christian activism, proclaiming it shameful that the liturgy was the endowment of an elite and insisting that it must be democratized, that is, made nourishment for everyone, a living-out of baptism through worship and social action. In Austria there was the Augustinian monastery at Klosterneuburg, with Pius Parsch calling for a liturgical participation that was full and active, that connected liturgy and daily life.

Then there was the fascinating passage of the liturgical movement from Europe to the United States. Here the most prominent figure was a young Benedictine, Virgil Michel, who studied philosophy in Rome but immersed himself in the different schools of social, industrial, and economic ethics. Michel's thought was stimulated by Beauduin and his development of the doctrine of the Mystical Body. Michel traveled extensively in Italy, Germany, France, and Spain, living close to the people, observing daily life in monasteries and churches, discussing philosophy with philosophers, farming with farmers, and liturgy with liturgists. He saw the liturgical movement as a means of countering the secularism and individualism of the modern age. He recognized the role of women in the world and was concerned for the full and active participation of the laity in the liturgy. And happily, while absorbing all that Europe could offer, he made what he discovered as American as only an American mind could make it. He saw what none of the great masters in Europe seemed to see: the connection of social justice with a new social spirituality. For him, Leo XIII's labor encyclicals and Pius X's liturgical reforms did not happen within one generation by accident. They were responses to cries of the masses for Christ; they belonged together.

It was actually in the 1930s and 1940s that the connection be-tween liturgical and social reform became strong. It was then that liturgy became a significant concern for men and women involved in such movements as Catholic Action, the Catholic Worker, the Campion Propaganda Movement, Friendship House, the Grail Movement, and the Christian Family Move-ment.

There is an interesting point of disagreement among experts. Bryan Hehir found that in the 1940s and 1950s, the twentieth-century liturgical movement and social ministry in the United States enjoyed a close rapport. One of his first approaches to the systematic study of Catholic social teaching came through reading the *Proceedings* of the Liturgical Conference. There the names Diekmann, Hillenbrand, Sheehan, Reinhold, and Leonard complemented the names Ryan, Haas, Higgins, and Egan.[2] On the other hand, in a 1994 interview with Keith Pecklers, Jack Egan expressed his belief that the close rapport was the ideal more than the norm. Pecklers writes:

> [Those] who bridged the gap between the liturgical and social movements were relatively few. Many liturgical leaders missed the social justice aspect in their promotion of a liturgical revival, in Egan's estimation. Virgil Michel, H. A. Reinhold, and Reynold Hillenbrand were, of course, exceptions to this, in that they labored tirelessly for an integration of these two important dimensions of ecclesial life.[3]

A similar divergence rears its head where the Second Vatican Council is concerned. Hehir is convinced that the efforts of Michel and others, the encyclicals *Mystici Corporis* and *Mediator Dei,* and the social teachings of Leo XIII, Pius XI, and Pius XII bore fruit in Vatican II, e.g., in the Constitution on the Sacred Liturgy and the Pastoral Constitution on the Church in the Modern World. Hehir writes: "The Council provided the

---

[2] J. Bryan Hehir, "Foreword" to *Liturgy and Social Justice*, ed. Mark Searle (Collegeville: The Liturgical Press, 1980) 9.

[3] Interview of John Egan by Keith Pecklers, December 15, 1994, DePaul University, Chicago; as reported by Peckers, *The Unread Vision,* 149, n. 184.

framework for the diverse movements of the 1940s and 1950s
to become central strands in the fabric of Catholic faith at the
level of theological reflection and Christian life."[4] On the other
hand, Margaret Kelleher notes that:

> One looks in vain throughout the Constitution on the Liturgy
> . . . to find an explicit connection made between the liturgy and
> social reform. . . . The famous statement identifying liturgy as
> "the summit toward which the activity of the Church is di-
> rected" and "the fount from which all her power flows" (SC 10)
> was a perfect context for making a connection between liturgy
> and the work of justice, but this was not done.[5]

She further comments:

> In reflecting on the missed connection on the occasion of the
> twentieth anniversary of *Sacrosanctum Concilium* John Egan
> suggested that there were too few people who had really seen the
> liturgy as a source and paradigm for social reform and that
> the impact made by those who did was minimal. His reading
> of the situation in the United States was that cooperation be-
> tween the liturgical apostolate and the social apostolate had
> virtually disappeared by the late 1950s. Thus it was not part of
> the planning before the council and "liturgy and justice went
> their own ways during and after the council."[6]

What is generally recognized is that the intimate link between liturgy and social justice, Michel's vision of liturgy as
"the indispensable basis of Christian social regeneration"[7] is
a "potential largely unfulfilled in the Church in the United
States."[8] In large measure, liturgists and social activists occupy

[4] Hehir, 10.

[5] Margaret M. Kelleher, "Liturgy and Social Transformation: Exploring
the Relationship," *U.S. Catholic Historian* 16 (Fall 1998) 64.

[6] Ibid. The quotation from John Egan is from his *Liturgy and Justice: An
Unfinished Agenda* (Collegeville: The Liturgical Press, 1983) 5; also printed
in *Origins* (September 22, 1983) 245–53.

[7] Virgil Michel, "The Liturgy the Basis of Social Regeneration," *Orate
Fratres* 9 (1935) 545.

[8] Hehir, 10.

two separate camps, and our Catholic people are tragically un-aware that in the Catholic vision liturgy and justice belong to-gether, that one without the other is not completely Catholic. My purpose at this point is to suggest why it is simply impera-tive that the link be restored.

II. We turn now to Scripture. Why? Because a constant theme in Scripture is justice. Almost a quarter century ago, Scripture scholar John R. Donahue shaped a working definition of bibli-cal justice with admirable succinctness:

> In general terms the biblical idea of justice can be described as *fidelity to the demands of a relationship.* In contrast to modern indi-vidualism the Israelite is in a world where "to live" is to be united to others in a social context either by bonds of family or by covenant relationships. This web of relationships—king with people, judge with complainants, family with tribe and kinfolk, the community with the resident alien and [with the] suffering in their midst and all with the covenant God—constitutes the world in which life is played out.[9]

Fidelity to relationships that stem from a covenant. Within that context, in what sense is God just? Because God always acts as God should, that is, invariably faithful to God's prom-ises: "the faithful God who keeps His merciful covenant down to the thousandth generation toward those who love Him and keep His commandments, but . . . makes the person who hates him personally pay for it" (Deut 7:9-10).[10] God's fidelity was touchingly revealed when God's people lamented, "The Lord has forsaken me; my Lord has forgotten me." To which the Lord responded, "Can a mother forget her infant, be without tenderness for the child of her womb? Even should she forget,

---

[9] John R. Donahue, "Biblical Perspectives on Justice," *The Faith that Does Justice: Examining the Christian Sources for Social Change,* ed. John C. Haughey (New York: Paulist Press, 1977) 69 (italics in text). For a more complete presentation of biblical justice than is possible in a single lecture, see my *Preaching the Just Word* (New Haven, Conn.: Yale University Press, 1996) 1–26.

[10] Scripture citations are taken from the NAB.

I will never forget you. See, upon the palms of my hands I have written your name" (Isa 49:14-16).

When were Israelites just? They were just when they were in right relation in all aspects of their life: properly postured toward God, toward other men and women, and toward the earth, God's material creation. Love God above all else; love every man, woman, and child like another self, as an image of God; touch God's nonhuman creation, all that is not God or the human person, with reverence, not as despot but as steward.

The social dimension of Scripture is evident on its very first page, the song of creation. Our incredibly imaginative God did not have in mind isolated units, autonomous entities, scattered disparately around a globe, basically independent each of every other. God had in mind a people, a human family, a community of persons, a body genuinely one. That divine idea began to take concrete shape when God brought an oppressed mass out of Egypt. The Exodus was not simply a liberation from slavery; it was the formation of a new social order, a contrast society. Not simply *freedom from,* but *freedom for:* freedom to form a community that would live under the covenant.

Moreover, it is not exploitation that the Hebrew term "have dominion" (Gen 1:26) mandates. "The Hebrew term is used in other places to describe the royal care that characterizes a king as God's vice-regent (Pss 72:8; 110:2; see also Ps 8:5-9). Like ancient kings, men and women are to be the mediators of prosperity and well-being. . . . Reverential care for God's creation rather than exploitation is the mandate given humanity in this section of Genesis."[11]

It is the Israelite tradition on justice that sparked the ministry of Jesus—that ministry he synthesized in the synagogue of his hometown Nazareth: "The Spirit of the Lord is upon me,

---

[11] John R. Donahue, *What Does the Lord Require? A Bibliographical Essay on the Bible and Social Justice* (revised and expanded) (St. Louis, Mo.: Institute of Jesuit Sources, 2000) 14. See also Dennis Olson, "God the Creator: Bible, Creation, Vocation," *Dialog: A Journal of Theology* 36 (Summer 1997) 173–74: The very context "suggests that this human dominion is to be carried out 'in the image of God,' an image that suggests nurture, blessing, and care rather than exploitation, abuse, and subjugation."

because [the Lord] has anointed me to bring glad tidings to the poor. He has sent me to proclaim liberty to captives and recovery of sight to the blind, to let the oppressed go free" (Luke 4:18).

Here is a suggestion. Some disenchanted evening, thumb through Mark's Gospel. Without speaking specifically of justice, Jesus is constantly dealing with the reality, struggling to make all relationships right. His miracles are not primarily a proof of Jesus' power. For the leper is not only cured; a human person ostracized from society, severed from the synagogue, and banished to the edge of his city is restored to his family and his community (Mark 1:40-45). A paralytic is not simply loosed of his paralysis; he is restored to God's friendship: "Your sins are forgiven" (Mark 2:5). Jesus makes a withered hand whole on the Sabbath, to stress a right relationship to God: "The Sabbath was made for men and women, not women and men for the Sabbath" (Mark 2:27). A wild man is not only freed from an unclean spirit; Jesus sits with him, talks to him, listens to him; and when he wants to stay with Jesus, Jesus sends him home to his family (Mark 5:1-20).

When his disciples argue, centuries before Mohammed Ali, about who's the greatest, Jesus shows that their role in his work is one of service. He takes into his arms a little child, an example then of a social nobody—no status, no social significance—and presents the child as a symbol of the *anawim*, the poor in spirit, the lowly in the Christian community: "Whoever receives one child such as this in my name receives me" (Mark 9:37).

Take the widow and her two small coins (Mark 12:41-44). For years I have recognized that in dropping into the temple treasury all she had to live on, "by the totality of her self-giving," she was foreshadowing "the complete self-giving of Jesus on the cross."[12] Instructed by insightful scholars, I now see Jesus lamenting "the tragedy of the day."[13] This widow had

---

[12] Mario DiCicco, "What Can One Give in Exchange for One's Life? A Narrative-Critical Study of the Widow and Her Offering, Mark 12:41-44," *Currents in Theology and Mission* 25 (1998) 446.

[13] Joseph A. Fitzmyer, *The Gospel According to Luke (X–XXIV)* (Garden City, N.Y.: Doubleday, 1985) 1321.

been encouraged by religious leaders to give as she did. Jesus condemned the value system that motivated her action—a poor widow persuaded by the hierarchy of her religion to plunk into the treasury her last penny. It was Jesus' quiet but passionate rebuke to a structure of sin; he was condemning a social injustice.

What, then, is the difference between biblical justice and other forms of justice rooted in the philosophical tradition: commutative justice, distributive justice, social justice? Here, John Donahue has been instructive:

(1) Biblical justice does not permit a strict philosophical definition; in the texts it is often linked with qualities such as mercy, steadfast love, and fidelity. "The traditional contrast between obligations in charity and obligations in justice is foreign to the Bible."

(2) Fundamentally, biblical justice is *making things right,* "not simply recognizing or defining *individual rights."* Its concern is the right relation of human beings to God and to one another. "There is no conflict between the 'vertical dimension,' that is, the proper relationship to God and God's commands, and the 'horizontal dimension,' the need to structure social life in a way that respects human dignity and is concerned for the vulnerable in the community."

(3) Biblical justice is neither "blind" nor totally impartial. "It is partial to those most affected by evil and oppression," symbolized in the Old Testament by widows, orphans, the poor, and strangers. It is "embodied in the NT by Jesus' mission to those on the social and religious margin of society."[14]

I am delighted by Donahue's summation: "There are 'two women of justice,' one with a scale and her eyes blinded, and the other, who proclaims: '[H]e has shown might with his arm, dispersed the arrogant of mind and heart. He has thrown down rulers from their thrones, but lifted up the lowly. The hungry he has filled with good things, the rich he has sent away empty' (Luke 1:51-53)."[15]

[14] Donahue, *What Does the Lord Require?* 28.
[15] Ibid.

III. Finally, the third and most significant area: liturgical theology. How might biblical justice invigorate our liturgies, and how might our liturgies help fashion a people of God's own justice? I begin with a basic fact: The justice the liturgy celebrates transcends the ethical and the legal. Mark Searle put it succinctly twenty-one years ago: "The liturgy celebrates the justice of God himself, as revealed by him in history, recorded in the Scriptures, and proclaimed in the assembly of the faithful."[16]

But precisely how? Recently I declared that the liturgy does not supply us with practical wisdom in the social, political, and economic arenas. I now retract that error. If the homily is liturgy, if, as Vatican II declared, the homily is "part of the liturgical action,"[17] then a well-prepared homilist can, indeed should, link the Gospel to what is going on in politics, in a nation with a surplus in the trillions, and in the moral climate of society as a whole. Still, a basic question remains: How does the Liturgy of the Eucharist as a whole shape us into people who can recognize justice or injustice when we see it, stimulate us to live justly ourselves individually and as a Church, to practice justice, to denounce, diminish, even destroy injustice?

Recall that the liturgy, specifically the Eucharist, is the very presence of Jesus, the Servant of justice, in the people assembled, in the Word proclaimed, in the Body and Blood shared. Recall that biblical justice is a matter of relationships. And what are these relationships? There are three—to God, to people, to the earth.

The Eucharist reveals and celebrates our relationship to *God.* Here I confess my daily displeasure as I reach the Eucharistic prayer and I am instructed to pray, "We do well" to give God thanks and praise. "We do well": a dreadful translation or substitution for the old Latin "Vere dignum et iustum est." To praise God and thank God always and everywhere "is utterly fitting and a matter of justice." If I do not praise and thank God regularly, constantly, I am unfaithful to my covenant with God cut in the blood of Christ; I am guilty of biblical injustice.

---

[16] Mark Searle, "Serving the Lord with Justice," in *Liturgy and Social Justice,* 15–16.

[17] SC 35. See also SC 52: "part of the liturgy itself."

Why are praise and thanks a matter of justice? Because it is God to whom we owe our being, our existence, our life at every moment. Because it is God to whom we owe our salvation in Christ. Because it is "God's love [of us]" that "has been poured out into our hearts through the Holy Spirit that has been given to us" (Rom 5:5). Because it is God who is our last end, our hope, our destiny.

The Eucharist reveals and celebrates our relationship with *one another.* Once more Mark Searle has ventured a fresh perspective: In the Eucharist "We stand to one another not as the rich to the poor, the wise to the ignorant, the strong to the needy, the clever to the simple; we stand rather as the poor to the poor, the weak to the weak, the loved to the loved."[18] In 1981, Robert Hovda expressed in striking syllables the equalizing, leveling power of the Eucharist:

> Where else [other than at Eucharist] in our society are all of us—not just a gnostic elite—called to be social critics, called to extricate ourselves from the powers and principalities that claim to rule our daily lives in order to submit ourselves to the sole dominion of the God before whom all of us are equal? Where else in our society are we all addressed and sprinkled and bowed to and incensed and touched and kissed and treated like *somebody*—all in the very same way? Where else do economic czars and beggars get the same treatment? Where else are food and drink blessed in a common prayer of thanksgiving, broken and poured out, so that everybody, *everybody* shares and shares alike?[19]

Wondrously true, but even there we cannot help experiencing a torment and a tension.[20] The liturgical assembly does not adequately reflect the justice of the kingdom; it reflects more obviously the divisions of social groupings. For all our eucha-

---

[18] Searle, "Serving the Lord with Justice," 23–24.

[19] I have not yet discovered the precise source of this quotation. I first discovered it on a memorial card for Fr. Hovda and recently found part of the same idea in an article of his, "The Vesting of Liturgical Ministers," *Worship* 54 (1980) 98–117 at 105.

[20] See Searle, "Serving the Lord with Justice," 25–26.

ristic equality, the tensions abide: rich and poor and the in-between, black and white and yellow and red and brown, men and women, the famous and the forgotten, CEOs and cleaning folk and the unemployed, Anglos and Hispanics, and all the rest. How can the liturgy affect such divisions? How build up the single body of Christ that Godfrey Diekmann rightly insists was the soul of the pre-Vatican II pastoral-liturgical movement, the one image he believes can inspire us to grasp and live what it means to share the life of God?[21]

Many years ago, a Jesuit colleague of mine at the Woodstock Theological Center in Washington, D.C., John C. Haughey (now at Loyola University Chicago), recaptured for me an unforgettable insight expressed by government people engaged in a Woodstock project on government decision making. As they saw it, good liturgy facilitates public responsibility, not because it provides principles of solution, that is, tells people precisely what to think about specific conflicts; rather because a celebrant who effectively celebrates the transcendent puts them in touch with that which transcends all their burning concerns, their particular perplexities. Good liturgy frees them to sort out the issues they have to decide, because it makes them aware of their addictions and their illusions, casts a pitiless light on myopic self-interest, detaches from a narrow selfishness, facilitates Christian discernment. In that sense liturgy is not so much didactic as evocative. Let *God* transpire; let *God* speak!

I agree, with one clarification. The effectiveness of the eucharistic celebration is not limited to the priest celebrant who "effectively celebrates the transcendent." It is the whole assembly in its full, conscious, active participation that effectively celebrates the transcendent; hence, the significance of the double epiclesis: the invoking of the Holy Spirit on the people gathered and on the bread and wine, emphasizing not only the transformation of the elements into the Body and Blood of Christ, but the transformation of the community.

---

[21] See Patrick Marrin, "Diekmann Says Hold Fast to Hope," *National Catholic Reporter* (February 26, 1999) 11–12.

No, the eucharistic signs and symbols do not of themselves change social, political, and economic structures, do not speak directly to complex issues of poverty and racism, of statecraft and technology. But they should change untold hearts and minds, grace them to admit the oppressions for which they may be responsible, inspire them to struggle with others for the coming of a kingdom characterized by peace and justice and love.[22]

The liturgy reveals and celebrates our relationship to the *earth*, to material creation. God's "things" can be used to build up relationships or destroy them—from a jug of wine to nuclear energy, from bread shared generously to luxuries clutched feverishly. The breaking of the one Bread, our sharing in the one Christ, cries out against the way we turn God's creation committed to our care into captives of our cupidity—yes, into weapons of power and destruction. Again, not specific solutions, but new hearts, new minds.

I have focused on the Eucharist, but the pertinent symbols in liturgy are not limited to bread and wine. There is the water, simultaneously symbolic of death and of birth. There is the oil for healing, the oil for consecration, the oil for faith building. There is the wood of the cross, supreme paradox of life through death, symbol of reconciliation with God and neighbor, of discipleship. There is the incense rising to heaven for forgiveness, for veneration, for exorcism. There is the ring, symbol of love and fidelity. There is darkness and there is light.[23]

Still on the "things" of God, I have been stimulated by an intriguing ambiguity uncovered by Fordham University's Elizabeth Johnson. It concerns the age-old expression *communio sanctorum*. The word *sanctorum* could mean either "holy persons" or "holy things," participation in sacred realities, especially the

---

[22] In these last two paragraphs, I am borrowing from a section on preaching justice in my *Preaching: The Art and the Craft* (New York/Mahwah: Paulist Press, 1987) 130.

[23] See the fine articles by Stephen Happel, both entitled "Symbol," in *The New Dictionary of Theology*, eds. Joseph A. Komonchak, et al. (Wilmington, Del.: Michael Glazier, 1987) 996–1002; and in *The New Dictionary of Sacramental Worship*, ed. Peter E. Fink (Collegeville: The Liturgical Press, 1990) 1237–45.

eucharistic bread and the cup of salvation, the meaning when the phrase was first used in the Eastern Church. Medieval theologians, she notes, "played with both meanings." Actually, "there is no need to choose between the two for they reinforce one another." And then Johnson's insight into a profound application today:

> In the light of the contemporary moral imperative to treat the evermore damaged earth as a sacred creation with its own intrinsic rather than instrumental value, the elusive quality of the phrase's original meaning is a happy circumstance. At its best, sacramental theology has always drawn on the connection between the natural world and the signs of bread, wine, water, oil, and sexual intercourse which, when taken into the narrative of Jesus' life, death, and resurrection, become avenues of God's healing grace. Now, in the time of earth's agony, the sancta can be pushed to its widest meaning to include the gifts of air, water, land, and the myriad creatures that share the planet with human beings in interwoven ecosystems—the brothers and sisters of Francis of Assisi's vision. For the universe itself is the primordial sacrament through which we participate in and communicate with divine mystery. Since the same divine Spirit who lights the fire of the saint also fuels the vitality of all creation, then "communion in the holy" includes holy people and a holy world in interrelationship. By this line of thinking, a door opens from within the symbol of the communion of saints itself to include all beings, sacred bread and wine certainly, but also the primordial sacrament, the earth itself. Once again, this symbol reveals its prophetic edge as its cosmic dimension calls forth an ecological ethic of restraint of human greed and promotion of care for the earth.[24]

IV. Conclusion. There are other ways of approaching the relationship between worship and justice. John Coleman, for example, has submitted seven ways is which Eucharist is essentially a proclamation of social justice.[25] I have submitted an

[24] Elizabeth A. Johnson, "Community on Earth as in Heaven: A Holy People and a Sacred Earth Together," Santa Clara Lectures 5, no. 1 (Santa Clara, Calif.: Santa Clara University, 1998) 13.

[25] See John A. Coleman, "How the Eucharist Proclaims Social Justice," *Church* 16 (Winter 2000) 5–9 and *Church* 17 (Spring 2001) 11–15.

approach which has the advantage of linking liturgy specifically with *biblical* justice, and therefore with *all* of our relationships: to God, to every human person, and to material creation.
Now I offer a set of conclusions directly related to the issue at
hand: liturgy and justice reunited.

We are servants of justice—but only if we do not sever social
action from the most powerful source of grace at our command. Only if we and our people recognize that our self-giving
to God's justice draws its power from a sacred hour, from the
Servant who still proclaims to the world in and through us,
"This is my body given for you" (Luke 22:19). Only if, as suffering servants, we are prepared to walk the way of the cross
that is inseparable from proclaiming God's justice, prepared to
follow the Servant who "was despised and rejected by others,
a man of sorrows, one from whom others hide their faces"
(Isa 53:3).

In season and out of season, I shall continue to insist that
social activists and practitioners of God's justice on the one
hand, and liturgists and worshipers at God's liturgy on the
other hand, dare not constitute two utterly separate organizations, especially two constituencies in conflict. How can expert
liturgists and devout worshipers claim to be men and women
of biblical justice if they do not live the words of Yahweh
through Isaiah?

> This, rather, is the fasting that I wish:
>   releasing those bound unjustly,
>   untying the thongs of the yoke;
> Setting free the oppressed,
>   breaking every yoke;
> Sharing your bread with the hungry;
>   sheltering the oppressed and the homeless;
> Clothing the naked when you see them,
>   and not turning your back on your own.
> Then your light shall break forth like the dawn,
>   and your wound shall quickly be healed. . . .
> Then you shall call, and the Lord will answer;
>   you shall cry for help, and He will say: Here I am.
>   (Isa 58:6-9)

And how can social-justice practitioners do justice to their activism if they draw their power from sheer human competence and energy, and not from the most efficacious, most dynamic source of grace in our universe—from the liturgy that Vatican II declared "is the source from which all [the Church's] power proceeds"?[26]

A final word. As you know, one of the living liturgical leaders long convinced that there is an intrinsic affinity between worshiping and living justly, that the liturgy itself is the pre-eminent school of justice, is Godfrey Diekmann.[27] He participated in the 1963 protest march on Washington, stood about fifty yards from Martin Luther King Jr. during the unforgettable "I Have a Dream" address. Despite the unhappiness of the then bishop of Mobile-Birmingham, Godfrey joined other priests in the 1965 march on Selma, Alabama. In fact, the banner he carried then continues to brighten his monastery room. It reads, "Selma is in Minnesota, too." Not himself a day-in-day-out social activist,

> Godfrey was one of a good number of liturgists caught in the crossfire of strategies of justice in the late sixties and early seventies [of the 20th century], an inevitable dispute given the early liturgical movement's presumption that a social agenda would be achieved by a *slow* and *organic* development, with the laity gradually becoming empowered through liturgy to assume their position as leaders in the marketplace. This strategy, according to Andrew Greeley, became unsatisfactory to promoters of justice. Instead of waiting for the liturgy to transform the laity, priests took over! Liturgical activities of the fifties promised great results if liturgy were modernized—but no one dreamt how far things would go, and there was no structure in place, in terms of artists, musicians, scholars, resources at every level. "We need to realize," Greeley concluded, "that transformation

[26] SC 10.

[27] See the splendid biography by Kathleen Hughes, *The Monk's Tale: A Biography of Godfrey Diekmann, O.S.B.* (Collegeville: The Liturgical Press, 1991), specifically 277–82.

is going to take a long, long time. Social activists demand short-term results; what Godfrey was predicting is necessarily long-term."[28]

I can only hope and pray that the vision of this common-sense nonagenarian may prevail, may draw together once again our liturgists and social reformers. Not primarily to establish a single fraternity; rather that the Body of Christ may move more effectively from Church to world, from altar to people, from Christ crucified on Calvary to Christ crucified at the crossroads of our earth. Only then will we realize, bring to concrete actuality, what a perceptive Protestant put into a penetrating expression: "If you Catholics could get your act together, you'd be dangerous!"[29]

[28] Ibid., 282 (italics in text). The Greeley material is from a taped interview dated November 24, 1987.

[29] The second and third sections of this essay stem in large measure, but with some significant revisions and additions, from my Diekmann Lecture at St. John's University, Collegeville, Minnesota, April 22, 1999, published in *Worship* 73 (1999) 386–98.

John P. Hogan

People of Faith and Global Citizens: Eucharist and Globalization

My topic is the immense one of relating Eucharist to globalization, the dominant problematic of our new century, and in turn some of the corresponding implications for economic and environmental justice. Given the breadth of the issue, I have chosen to look at the foundation of Eucharist and how it relates to globalization. This approach was prompted by Langdon Gilkey's comment that "the Eucharist needs no redirection . . . it is the center; but it needs . . . an infinite widening and extension over the whole earth."[1]

My approach has been formed from two perspectives. The first is my own career, which has focused on third world development issues in a rapidly globalizing economy. The second has to do with the crystallizing debate around the linkage between Eucharist and justice. My steps in pursuit of that linkage were quickened by Kathleen Hughes' pointed question, "When Jesus said, 'Do this in memory of me,' what was the *this* he had in mind?"[2] John Coleman reminds us that social justice finds its roots in and is fed by the eucharistic imagination, and asks,

---

[1] Langdon Gilkey, "Symbols, Meaning, Divine Presence," *Theological Studies* 35 (June 1974) 266–67.

[2] Kathleen Hughes, *The Liturgy that Does Justice,* Preaching the Just Word video series (Chicago: Liturgy Training Publications, 1995).

"How then have we so lost our way that such claims can seem provocative?"[3] Eucharist is the essence of Christian praxis, the fulfillment of baptism, a thankful yes to Jesus' life, death, and resurrection which incorporates us as a spirited community to do as he did—seek and build the kingdom of God. Indeed, this understanding runs throughout our tradition. What went wrong? Could it be that we have let a too individualistic and therapeutic emphasis on "real presence" obscure the deeper meaning of Christ's presence and action in us as a community of believers? St. Augustine said, "We eat the body of Christ to become the body of Christ."[4] What in the world might that mean in 2001?

To a great extent, globalization has been a western big business and particularly, a U.S.-dominated process. However, that does not mean that if human concerns, and particularly concerns for the poor, are brought to the fore, a greater common good cannot come from the process. That is the message Pope John Paul II creatively set forth in "Ecclesia in America." In response to globalization, the Pope counter-proposed the "globalization of solidarity."[5]

Traces of all the received meanings of Eucharist, in the face of globalization, need to be teased out: global covenant community, thanksgiving, sacrifice, reconciliation, table ministry, and the banquet of human destiny. If a few little pieces of the globe, bread and wine, "fruit of the vine and work of human hands," can be Christ's presence, then so can the rest of the universe. As Michael Himes says, "The Eucharist is the tip of the iceberg. It is the first step in the transubstantiation of all creation . . . the destiny of the universe."[6]

[3] John A. Coleman, "How the Eucharist Proclaims Social Justice," Part One, *Church* (Winter 2000) 5 and Part Two, *Church* (Spring 2001) 11–15.

[4] Michael J. Himes, *Doing the Truth in Love: Conversations about God, Relationships and Service* (New York: Paulist Press, 1995) 118.

[5] John Paul II, "Ecclesia in America," *Origins* 28 (February 4, 1999) 566–92. See also John P. Hogan, "Ecclesia in America: Towards a Catechesis of Global Solidarity," *Living Light* 35 (Summer 1999) 16–27.

[6] Himes, 129. For anaphora, preface, and epiclesis, see *Catechism of the Catholic Church*, 34, no. 1353.

When and how does Eucharist call us to be open to the positive potential of the emerging global economy and culture? When and how might Eucharist be a real symbol of a needed resistance to a global homogenization of local cultures that desecrates the environment and discards human beings as "collateral damage" of economic "progress"? How might Eucharist provide the theological basis for Catholic social teaching on solidarity, subsidiarity, and the option for the poor? How might it be coupled with a discernment process that rests on the eucharistic imagination, builds community, and takes action on behalf of justice? With the dominant problematic of globalization in mind, the following will try to get to the "this" in Jesus' mandate.

St. Paul: Discerning the Body of Christ

How does Eucharist call us to stewardship and global solidarity with the poor? The New Testament is replete with stories of invitations to homes and fellowship meals. There were lots of dinner parties. At these affairs, Jesus constantly reminds his friends to be thankful. He also used such occasions to reach out to hookers and hustlers. Participants in the dinners and picnics are all treated as equals; all receive the same meal.

In like manner, Jesus' last meeting with his disciples was a meal of thanksgiving and blessing that stretched back to earlier covenants and particularly to the Passover from slavery. However, this time he changed the blessing before he broke the bread, saying, "This is my body." In effect, he was saying that this bread is not only a reminder of the Passover bread our ancestors ate, this bread is me. He announced that "this wine was his blood, the blood of the new covenant."[7] The participants in the new covenant became blood relatives, not only of Jesus but of one another, and with that comes responsibility for the extended family. The new covenant has demanding terms, which are laid out in John's Gospel, when the Master washes his disciples' feet. He reverses the whole social order and scandalizes his closest followers, especially Peter.

[7] Himes, 124–25.

Turning to St. Paul's treatment of the eucharistic celebration in 1 Corinthians 11:17-34, I look to the work of John Haughey. The lessons to be learned from Paul clearly apply to our task. Here Paul is seeking to get to the root of the insensitive behavior of the Corinthians. He aims for the deeper meaning of the "real presence" as the Body of Christ identified with the community. "Defective perception of the mystery of the Lord's presence in the community led to defective internalization, and, in turn, to deficient projection or social behavior."[8] The Corinthians, in spite of their belief in the Real Presence, didn't get it. Their understanding was very much tied up with an "individuated Christ," in that there was little or no grasp of "being members of one another in a whole which is his sacred presence. . . ."[9] Paul's concern gets behind interpersonal behavior as well as racial, national, economic, ideological, and social divisions. Maybe we still suffer from the Corinthian myopia.

Had the Corinthians understood Eucharist as the presence that unites members in the body and creates a single entity, they would have realized how sacrilegious their behavior toward one another was. We can only imagine what it might have been toward non-Christians! "A nascent gnosticism was developing in Corinth which had some portion of the community of believers verticalizing and spiritualizing their faith in Christ."[10] This manifested itself both in inflated egos and lack of concern for the less educated, the stranger, the poor, and the slave. Then as now, Jesus' humanity seems to have posed more of a problem than his divinity.

Paul invites the Corinthians to a discernment process of self-examination around Eucharist. "Their sin was not a lack of faith in Jesus. . . . They were in error about who they were, because they were wrong about who he was now. Their belief was in a disembodied Jesus. They believed in one not bodied

[8] John C. Haughey, "Eucharist at Corinth: You are the Christ" in Thomas E. *Above Every Name: The Lordship of Christ and Social Systems,* ed. Thomas E. Clarke (Ramsey, N.J.: Paulist Press, 1980) 108.
[9] Ibid., 109.
[10] Ibid., 113.

the way he said he would be."[11] Paul reminds the community that Jesus said he would be there in the poor, the prisoner, and the foreigner, but Paul also raises the trinitarian dimension when he writes "that they all may be one in us" (John 17:21).

If the above textual reasoning is accurate, Jesus' mandate would then be: "Do this again and again by remembering me at your table fellowship. But you remember me if you know my presence with you is through one another whom I am fashioning into so many members of my own body."[12] In Paul's view, the private, individual possession of Christ comes at no cost and is selfish. Rather, he understood Eucharist as participation in a very concrete, communal way. Haughey refers to this as "relational wholeness," which makes us Christ's Body and members of one another: "The knitting together of individuals would be their redemption and at the same time would be the beginning of the recapitulation of all systems in Christ."[13]

This understanding of Eucharist offers intriguing food for thought for realizing Christ's presence on a global scale. Paul sees the concrete working out of real presence in a community of people who are open and identify not with the few but with all—with Christ himself in the whole body. But there is great movement and freedom within that body, precisely because "they were Christ's body."[14] To grasp what Paul seems to be saying is startling! Together we are Christ! We are one with the "social flesh" of the Word of God. Christ's death and resurrection can now become the determinants of our lives. If we are truly members of his body, he is now us.[15]

How should this view of Eucharist as "relational wholeness" affect us? To what does being one in the Spirit call us in relation to the emerging global system and the people in it, especially

[11] Ibid., 117.

[12] Ibid., 120. See Haughey, 118–20, where he refers to William F. Orr and James Arthur Walther, *1 Corinthians: A New Translation* (The Anchor Bible; Garden City, N.Y.: Doubleday, 1976) for discussion on the "uses of the neuter demonstrative this."

[13] Haughey, 123.

[14] Ibid., 125.

[15] Ibid., 127.

the poor? Should our corporate presence be a challenge to that other corporate presence? Paul's views touched political, economic, and environmental issues. He had profound respect for all created reality and was not afraid of the local, the social, the foreign, the body.

Clearly, this approach to eucharistic presence puts theological flesh on the theoretical bones of Catholic social teaching— solidarity, subsidiarity, and the option for the poor. It provides the "body"—head, hands, feet—for the Church as a transnational, global actor. It is a much more "real" presence than a privatized, individuated Jesus in a host. If we realize this "relational wholeness," we can be more effective in terms of global social ecological systems. But first, what kinds of situations might that body walk into?

Embodying the Globalization of Solidarity

In addressing the multicultural and multiracial aspects of the Western hemisphere in "Ecclesia in America," John Paul II bids us to travel three paths: to conversion, communion, and solidarity. The globalization of solidarity is the key to his vision. The term solidarity has a long history in Catholic social teaching. Theologically, it reflects the ontological unity of humankind redeemed as a new creation in Christ. It signifies the responsibility of all to stand with and promote human rights, economic and social development, and environmental concerns. It calls for a special commitment to those in need—in a very real sense, an identification with them. John Paul's linkage of solidarity with globalization is truly ingenious and a challenging call to American Catholics. The Church in America is called not only to promote greater integration between nations, thus helping to create an authentic globalized culture of solidarity, but also to cooperate with every legitimate means in reducing the negative effects of globalization, such as the domination of the powerful over the weak, especially in the economic sphere, and the loss of the values of local cultures in favor of a misconstrued homogenization.[16]

[16] "Ecclesia in America," no. 55. See Hogan, "Catechesis of Global Solidarity," 20.

Without defense of the poor and marginalized, both individuals and nations, globalization could end up being merely a new and perhaps more deadly form of colonialism. The Pope's analysis of global solidarity unfolds in light of foreign debt, corruption, drugs, the arms race, environmental degradation, racial and cultural discrimination, and immigration. These problems—the dehumanizing outcomes of a misguided economic globalization—lead to a culture of death where the powerful can relegate certain peoples to the dustbin of history.[17]

This is a direct challenge to the American Church, but what I find missing is a theological, sacramental, and liturgical base that unites the paths of conversion, communion, and solidarity. The path to solidarity would be greatly enhanced and supported theologically by applying Paul's notion of bodily eucharistic presence in the sense of "relational wholeness" to the community of believers and to the whole globe.

In order to understand better the current global context, especially from the perspective of the poor, I turn to a few snapshots of globalization from Africa and Latin America. I begin with a case study from Nigeria, "The Ogoni and Oil."[18] You hear the same story in every home you enter. You see it in every corner of the village you visit. The pitiable and scandalous tale is the same: "My once productive farmland," a farmer laments, "now lays fallow, barren—forever infertile. It is as though concrete has been poured over and cemented the surface of my means of livelihood. Large chunks of tar cover many of the farms." This predicament is not the plight of only the farmers in Ogoniland. The fishermen and women also suffer. The rivers are red, covered with "blood" from oil spills. The fish are dead or can no longer produce offspring.

The Ogoni are subsistence farmers and fishermen who live in the coastal delta of Nigeria, the area of the country's oil

[17] Ibid., no. 63. Hogan, 21.

[18] This case study is taken from the "Global Economy and Local Cultures" project ongoing at Woodstock Theological Center, Washington, D.C. The project works with Jesuit research centers around the world and is managed by Gasper LoBiondo, S.J.

production fields. Nigeria obtains ninety percent of its foreign earnings from oil and has contracted European and American firms to manage its oil fields. Oil pollution has had a devastating impact on the territory's agricultural land and rivers. The effect on families, children, and the work force has been disastrous. Neither government nor the corporations have done anything to improve conditions. Unemployment has increased; no hospitals, schools, water systems, or roads have been built. Employees of the foreign firms live in spacious quarters and employ Ogoni as servants. In spite of their oil-rich land, Ogoni men and women consider themselves a forsaken people. A popular saying in Nigeria, one which a person might say to an enemy, is "may oil be discovered in your backyard"—a blessing turned sour. Moreover, when a nonviolent movement was organized to address these concerns to the government, its leader was assassinated in 1995 by the president-dictator. Oil profits continue to flow out to Europe and the United States.

It is a sad parallel, but from the perspective of many African theologians, the extractive function of the oil industry in some ways mirrors the role of Eucharist. For instance, one could apply Cameroonian Jean-Marc Ela's comment on the Eucharist to the plight of the Ogoni: "The rigid rules on the eucharistic matter [legislating wheat bread and grape wine] oblige the African churches to 'resign themselves to being a tool for the prosperity of someone else's commerce.'"[19]

This case study can only hint at the tremendous complexity of the globalization process, as well as the devastating impact on family life, culture, and the environment. Since Americans, for the most part, are the winners in the globalization race, it is hard for us to hear that side of the story.

---

[19] Jean-Marc Ela, *African Cry* (Maryknoll, N.Y.: Orbis Books, 1980) 6; see ch. 1. See also Anselme Sanon, "Dimensions Antropologiques De L'Eucharistie," *La Documentation Catholique* (Aout 1981) 721–29; Tissa Balasuriyia, *The Eucharist and Human Liberation* (Maryknoll, N.Y.: Orbis Books, 1979); and Nicholas Paxton, "The Liberating Eucharist," *New Blackfriars* 64 (1983) 180–87; Leonardo Boff, *Los Sacramentos de la vida y la vida de los sacramentos,* Coleccion Iglesia Nueva, 19, 2nd ed. (Bogota: Indo-American Press Service, 1975).

To a great extent, our ability to identify with the poor and the local from our own context of affluence and the global is a eucharistic question. Unfortunately, our recent global track record has not been good; indeed some situations might indicate a failure of Eucharist. Consider Chile under Pinochet, Central America, Rwanda before and during the genocide, Northern Ireland and the Balkans.[20] All were situations where Eucharist became symbolic of division and exclusion rather than unity and inclusion. How many opportunities for reconciliation and forgiveness were missed? Perhaps when we look at our own issues of segregation, the plight of our cities, and tax structures, the global neglect of the poor comes closer to home. Paul's concerns are both local and global: "Examine yourself, and only then eat of the bread and drink of the cup. For all who eat and drink without discerning the body, eat and drink judgment against themselves" (1 Cor 11:28-31). If not properly discerned, Eucharist can be dangerous to our health!

In *Torture and Eucharist,* William T. Cavanaugh draws on the writings of Henri de Lubac and Gregory Dix to indicate the dire effects of an overly individualized concept of Eucharist. He comments that individuals are isolated and the Church is rendered ineffective in dealing with oppression, until an understanding of the "true" Body of Christ becomes present in the community. Only when this presence is lived in the community will the Church find the courage to stand up to torture.[21]

A renewed sense of Paul's embodied Eucharist is needed to infuse a global Catholicism capable of being incorporated in

---

[20] See, e.g., Karen Armstrong, *The Battle for God* (New York: Knopf, 2000); Mark Juergensmeyer, *Terror in the Mind of God* (Berkeley: Univ. of California Press, 2000) and *The New Cold War? Religious Nationalism Confronts the Secular State* (Berkeley: Univ. of California Press, 1993); and Woodstock Theological Center, *Forgiveness in Conflict Resolution: Reality and Utility—The Bosnian Experience* and *Forgiveness in Conflict Resolution: Reality and Utility—The Northern Ireland Experience* (Washington, D.C.: WTC, October 24 and June 18, 1997, respectively). Regarding the churches and the Rwanda genocide, see e.g., African Rights, *Rwanda: Death, Despair and Defiance* (London: African Rights, 1995 rev. ed.).

[21] William T. Cavanaugh, *Torture and Eucharist* (Oxford: Blackwell, 1998). See especially 205–07, 229–34, and 252ff.

each culture, yet open to the potential goods of a global culture. Robert Schreiter, in *The New Catholicity* for a global age,
calls for a theology of culture constructed on a foundation of
intercultural communication and hermeneutics.[22] He points
out that this theology of culture started with *Gaudium et Spes*
and has continued with John Paul II. Two central doctrines
provide key resources for such a theology of culture. The first
is the Trinity: "The missions of the Second and Third Persons
in the world, and God's reconciliation of the cosmos to the
divine Being are themes that take on new significance in a
globalized world." Second, the paschal mystery provides
Christians with a "master narrative" for an epoch without
master narratives. "The passion narrative itself brims with
post-colonial ironies of betrayal, denial, mistaken identifica-
tions, and abandonment. And it ends in great surprise."[23]

I fully agree with Schreiter on the importance of these two
themes for a theological response to globalization. However,
I would hasten to add Eucharist understood as a visible sign of
Christ's bodily presence expressing "relational wholeness." We
reenact *our* master narrative every Sunday. Without a broader
understanding of the central act of Christian worship, we run
the growing risk of aiding and abetting the growing separation
of the rich and poor—the Church of the rich and the Church of
the poor. Indeed, Eucharist is where Catholics are educated.

I close this section with a brief account of Eucharist as applied to globalization—in this case, resistance to globalization
because of its impact on the poor. This example comes from El
Salvador. Cavanaugh offers a cogent illustration of how and
when Eucharist might function as resistance to a negative globalization that compresses space and time and, under the pre-
tense of a united world, enslaves the poor. He quotes a homily
of Father Rutilio Grande of El Salvador.

> The Lord God gave us . . . a material world for all, without
> borders . . . "I'll buy half of El Salvador. Look at all my money.

[22] Robert J. Schreiter, *The New Catholicity: Theology between the Global and
the Local* (Maryknoll, N.Y.: Orbis Press, 1997) 130.
    [23] Ibid., 60.

That'll give me the right to it." . . . No! That's denying God!
. . . Christ has good reason to talk about his kingdom as a
meal. . . . [He] celebrated one the night before his supreme
sacrifice. . . . And he said that this was the great memorial of
the redemption: a table shared in brotherhood, where all have
their position and place.[24]

One month later, Grande was murdered. Archbishop Romero
declared, to the disgust of the rich and the military, that only
one Mass—the funeral Mass—would be celebrated in the archdiocese that Sunday. The elite was outraged. But Romero was
using the power of the Eucharist to collapse spatial barriers
separating rich and poor, not by simply declaring the Church
universal and united but rather by calling the faithful together
to one particular location around one altar and expressing the
Catholica in one place at one time.[25]

Hence, the Body of Christ has to be properly discerned;
otherwise, Christ is betrayed. This perhaps helps to explain
something of the failures of Eucharist mentioned above. In the
face of globalization, the body might call for support or resistance, depending on local circumstances. If our eucharistic
celebrations are to have anything to say to our new global situation, they will have to be accompanied by a reflective communal discernment process.

Critical Discernment and Relational Wholeness

The jury is still out as to whether globalization will prove a
blessing or curse to humanity. Thus far, however, it has had a

[24] William T. Cavanaugh, "The World in a Wafer: A Geography of the
Eucharistic as Resistance to Globalization," *Catholicism and Catholicity:
Eucharistic Communities in Historical and Contemporary Perspectives,* ed.
Sarah Beckwith (Oxford: Blackwell, 1999) 85. See also "Bishop Threatens
President with Excommunication" in *Houston Catholic Worker* 31 (May–
June 2001) 1 and 8. Bishop Hesayne challenges the president of Argentina's
neo-liberal economic policies that crush the poor and indicates the insin-
cerity of many communicants by alluding to the street-term "host-eaters."
[25] Cavanaugh, "World in a Wafer," 82. See James R. Brockman, *Romero:
A Life* (Maryknoll, N.Y: Orbis Books, 1989) 9–18.

killing effect on the world's poor, local cultures, and the environment. In a sense globalization has become a liturgy writ-large—with matching vestments, rituals, music, drama, food, and text. It has its rubrics, hierarchy, acolytes, and parishioners—only the poor are left out.

What I propose is an understanding of Eucharist with a corresponding discernment process that allows, even compels, the believing community to become aware, get involved, and exert influence on the globalization problematic, with its implications for economic and environmental issues. The "relational wholeness" understanding of Eucharist provides the identity and work plan for us as a Church to travel the path of conversion, communion, and solidarity with the poor. Christ's presence is global; therefore, we as a community are global and should so act. In a very real sense, we should feel the suffering of the Ogoni! After all, to a great extent, their plight is generated by our oil consumption, but, more importantly, the Ogoni and we are one in Christ's Body.

Solidarity needs to be more than a principle and an attractive slogan. For it to really reflect the ontological unity of humankind redeemed in Christ, our embodiment in him and him in us needs to be preached and reflected on during liturgy, emphasized in the prayer of the faithful, and discussed in communal discernment sessions. Such discernment needs to include honest, open interreligious and intercultural dialogue. Whether we like it or not, "global" is in.[26] The Church's articulation of Christ's presence and uniqueness needs to move beyond the negative defensiveness of *Dominus Jesus*.[27]

"Eucharist makes real the presence of Christ both in the elements and in the body of believers."[28] The majority of Catholics would probably agree with the former but scratch their heads at the latter. For most of us, Eucharist is an interior retreat—a "spiritual" thing. A corollary of that is the virtual ab-

[26] Schreiter, *New Catholicity*, 11–27.

[27] Congregation for the Doctrine of the Faith, *Dominus Jesus: On the Unicity and Salvific Universality of Jesus Christ and the Church* (Vatican City: CDF, 2000).

[28] Cavanaugh, *Torture and Eucharist*, 205.

sence of liturgy and Eucharist in official Catholic social teaching, as well as the relatively recent separation of liturgy from social thought and activism.[29] Both are serious betrayals, not only of the liturgical movement but also of the New Testament and patristic traditions, which deny the Eucharist its rightful educational role.

Moreover, I contend that an inductive, practical discernment process has to be built into our eucharistic celebrations to bring out the communal, bodily nature of eucharistic presence and relates that presence to justice issues in the global age. We need to begin with the experience of the local community. How do we experience community? How do we experience globalization? How do others around us or across town or around the world experience it? How and why does being the Body of Christ call us to seek solidarity in this situation? Are we in need of conversion from our habits, way of life, way of thinking? How do we reflect on our own experience when we have pulled it together into a personal and communal story? How do we judge our story, our situation? Do we need to change? Can we act on our judgment? What action should we take?

The above is a shorthand version of Bernard Lonergan's familiar theological method: experience, understanding, judgment, and decision (action). It is not the only discernment process which could serve our purposes, but it is one that maps clearly the cognitive and hermeneutical process and has been put to excellent use in examining the globalization process at the Woodstock Theological Center in Washington, D.C.[30]

This process is akin to the discernment to which Paul was calling the Corinthians, but it is broadened to global horizons. In the Eucharist, we "put on Christ" and relive his story, and, in doing that, discover our own. This is what we are called to

---

[29] See Coleman, "How the Eucharist Proclaims Social Justice," 5, for a brief sketch of the liturgy-justice linkage set in motion by Virgil Michel, O.S.B.

[30] Woodstock uses the Ignatian exercises updated with the Lonergan methodology. For a summary of this approach, see "Theological Reflection: Woodstock's Way of Working," interview with James L. Connor, *Woodstock Report* (December 1992) 3–7.

do at every Eucharist. Outcomes of the process might take many forms: support for the United Nations, fair trade practices, and even one day, a global tax. At other times, it might mean aiding the resistance to a crass globalization process that tramples on local cultures and the poor. Decisional actions might run the gamut from advocacy to volunteer efforts, to parish twinning, to support for the Catholic Campaign for Human Development and Catholic Relief Services efforts.

Such an approach implemented within the context of eucharistic presence as "relational wholeness" could ignite communities to take up difficult socioeconomic questions. The stock market, the World Trade Organization, energy policy, sweatshops, AIDS, drugs, racial, religious and ethnic conflict, immigration, arms trade and global warming are defining our globe. Distance no longer cleanses dividends. Since Americans are so far the "winners," we need to understand our role as members of the Body of Christ and our responsibilities to the "losers." That might be what Augustine meant by "We eat the body of Christ to become the body of Christ."

Conclusion

I readily admit that this broadening of horizons is a tall order for pastors, liturgists, religious educators, and parishioners, but it seems to me absolutely necessary, given today's world. We take on Jesus' Body and relive his life every time we participate in the eucharistic liturgy. At the same time, we find ourselves in a world thrown together—culturally, religiously, economically, and environmentally. Unfortunately, as Haughey points out, we seem to continue to follow "a Christ who looks more like the one our Corinthian forebears concocted than the one Paul preached." We allow Paul the eschatological horizons pointing to the future but fail to see that "they are also political [social, economic, and environmental] vistas pointing to the present and to possibilities in the Christ mystery we have even stopped imagining."[31]

---

[31] Haughey, 111.

Together—globe-wide—we are the Christ, members of one another. The problems of the Ogoni, as well as, say, the poor of Camden, New Jersey, are our problems as well. I am convinced that for the overwhelming majority of Catholics, education to solidarity, subsidiarity, and the option for the poor will not happen unless it takes place within the context of Eucharist— "The whole of Catholic praxis is training in sacramental vision."[32] These are uncharted waters, but eucharistic liturgy provides a compass pointing to the "infinite widening and extension over the whole earth" that Gilkey mentioned.

Christ's eucharistic bodily presence allows us to take risks and calls us to these tasks. As Gustavo Gutierrez reminds us, "the Church should rise to the demands of the moment." He adds wryly, "Some chapters of theology can be written only afterwards."[33]

[32] Michael J. Himes and Kenneth R. Himes, *Fullness of Faith: The Public Significance of Theology* (New York: Paulist Press, 1993) 113. At their June 2001 meeting, the U.S. Bishops drafted and adopted a statement, *The Real Presence of Jesus Christ in the Sacrament of the Eucharist: Basic Questions and Answers* (Washington, D.C.: USCC, 2001). The statement emphasizes the theory of "transubstantiation" and is apparently a response to concerns raised by a survey about "real presence" in the eucharistic bread and wine. There is only brief mention of Christ's presence in the scriptural word and "assembly" (no. 13).

[33] Gustavo Gutierrez, *A Theology of Liberation: History, Politics and Salvation* (Maryknoll, N.Y.: Orbis Books, 1973) 272.

| Bro. David Andrews, C.S.C.

The Lord's Table, the World's Hunger: Liturgy, Justice, and Rural Life

The National Catholic Rural Life Conference (NCRLC) was founded seventy-seven years ago by laypeople, religious men and women, priests, and bishops. In the library at St. Louis University, Father Edwin Vincent O'Hara initiated the movement on Catholic rural life.[1] In 1956 Archbishop O'Hara was on his way to an International Congress of Pastoral Liturgy at Assisi, Italy, when he died en route in Milan. When asked for his opinion of O'Hara, Father Louis Putz, C.S.C., a champion for the rights of the poor and the elderly, replied, "He was in my opinion one of the outstanding sponsors of social legislation in this country."[2] O'Hara pioneered legislation on the minimum wage, advocated for housing and care for the unemployed, and espoused such rural reforms as cooperatives, credit unions, and domestic support for farmers. O'Hara was a liturgical reformer and a social reformer. He was concerned with bringing about a greater conscious awareness and active participation of Catholics in worship and in the mission of justice. He saw a relationship between liturgy, justice, and rural life, between the hunger for God, justice, and the integrity of creation.

[1] J. G. Shaw, *Edwin Vincent O'Hara: American Prelate* (New York: Farrar, Straus, Cudahy, 1957) 261.
[2] Timothy Dolan, *Some Seeds Fell on Good Ground* (Washington, D.C.: The Catholic University of America Press, 1992).

In the 1930s Msgr. Luigi Ligutti became NCRLC's president and executive secretary. With the support of the Roosevelt administration, Ligutti founded a highly successful rural community development project in Granger, Iowa. He developed the project based upon Catholic social teaching, and he believed that ethnic and religious diversity would be key to success. Thus, he invited Catholics, Protestants, and mixed-marriage families to participate. In addition, he invited Italians, Germans, and Croatians to become founding family members. Each family received some acreage for their own food production, and a building was constructed for the community to come together.

This year marks the sixtieth anniversary of the naming of Ligutti as executive director of NCRLC. Ligutti was eventually to write sections of encyclicals (i.e., John XXIII's *Mater et Magistra*), to be the Vatican's voice at the Food and Agriculture Organization of the United Nations in Rome, and to found other projects for agricultural development around the world, including Agri Missio. He also helped to found the Pontifical Council for Justice and Peace. Ligutti published more than a dozen leaflets and brochures concerning the relationship between liturgy and the land.[3] Early on Ligutti was a supporter of women's roles in rural life as a friend of the Grail. He helped find the farm that was to become Grailville in Loveland, Ohio. In San Francisco in 1945, his was one of the few Catholic voices that sounded on behalf of the organization of the United Nations. One observer noted in 1973: "It would be safe to say that there would be no presence of the Catholic Church in any aspect of the work of the United Nations were it not for the important and decisive role played by Monsignor Ligutti."[4]

Other visionary leaders in the early days of Catholic Rural Life included Dorothy Day, Peter Maurin, Virgil Michel, O.S.B., John Rawe, S.J., John LaFarge, S.J., and Howard Bishop. To illustrate the contributions of these leaders, we can look to the work of Dorothy Day and Peter Maurin, founders of Catholic Worker.

[3] Vincent Yzermands, *The People I Love* (Collegeville: The Liturgical Press, 1976).

[4] Ibid., 75.

Catholic Worker in collaboration with NCRLC developed Catholic worker farms, where social thought and action, co-operative agricultural labor, and liturgy were combined. One such farm is in Marlboro, New York.

We can also look to contributions of Virgil Michel, pioneer of the American liturgical movement. He implemented in every way at his command the impulse that leads from participation in worship to involvement in the search for peace and justice. In 1935 Michel asked, "Can the liturgy help to give jobs or raise wages?"[5] To answer this question, he reviewed the dangers of individualism and collectivism, and offered a solution of moderation—a Christian spirit that takes into account both the individual and the social sides of human nature.[6] Michel followed the lead of Pope Pius XI, who stated in his 1931 encyclical *Quadregesimo anno* that "social reconstruction must be preceded by a profound renewal of the Christian spirit."[7] And where does a Christian turn to find the source of this Christian spirit? Michel's answer was the liturgy.

The basic idea of the liturgy, Michel argued, is rooted in the doctrine of the Mystical Body of Christ, which teaches interdependence of all members of the Church. With Christ as the head, this body, the Church, "is the highest type of Christian solidarity—a supernatural living solidarity or fellowship—not only in theory but also in practice."[8] Michel was confident that since liturgical worship is a "'visible united action on the part of the members'" of the Church, the members "'cannot fail to revive and foster in them a determination to carry their Christ-life into the social and economic sphere.'"[9] Michel's fundamental framework was to see the Mystical Body and active Christian cooperation as the basis for fostering a consciousness

[5] Virgil Michel, "The Liturgy: the Basis of Social Regeneration," *Orate Fratres* 9 (1935) 540.

[6] R. W. Franklin and Robert Spaeth, *Virgil Michel: American Catholic* (Collegeville: The Liturgical Press, 1988) 14.

[7] Robert Spaeth, *The Social Question: Essays on Capitalism and Christianity* (Collegeville: The Liturgical Press, 1987) 10.

[8] Michel, 541–42.

[9] Ibid., 545, quoting, Christopher Dawson.

within the body of believers that this life extends to shaping the reign of Christ in the world.

Michel, Ligutti, Day, O'Hara, and many others saw the connections between liturgy and justice in rural America. Their advocacy for an integral vision bore fruit in many areas, including pastoral letters, papal encyclicals, and Christian activity. Their vision forms the infrastructure for contemporary social action in rural areas by Catholic leaders, among others. For instance, Rick Dove, the Neuse Riverkeeper for seven years, has testified before the U.S. Congress about the harmful effects on humans and wildlife from hog pollution in North Carolina. He has participated in more than four thousand news stories on the impact of hog pollution on the rivers of North Carolina. Presently, he is challenging Smithfield, owner of the largest pork processing plant in North Carolina, by seeking to have federal law enforced to prevent the creation of hog waste lagoons. Clarence and Caroline Bormann of Bode, Iowa, were rural life directors for their diocesan deanery under the leadership of Father John Cain, a long-time leader in rural life concerns. The Bormanns filed suit in 1994 to negate their county supervisor's agricultural zoning, in an effort to oppose the construction of a large hog factory farm next door to their family farm. At eighty years of age, the Bormanns saw their case appealed to the U.S. Supreme Court. The National Pork Producers Council and the Farm Bureau had put together a large fund to fight the case. The Supreme Court ruled in favor of the Bormanns, striking down the Iowa's nuisance suit immunity, which would have protected the hog factory farm. In the case of Percy Schmeiser, a fourth-degree Knight of Columbus in Saskatchewan, a Canadian court found that he violated a Monsanto patent when he allegedly allowed genetically modified canola to be grown on his property without informing Monsanto. Schmeiser has been ordered to pay Monsanto thousands of dollars; he is trying to raise funds for an appeal.

Rick Dove, the Bormanns, and Percy Schmeiser. These Catholic voices, brought up on liturgical experiences linked to social justice concerns, have been willing to be contemporary Davids and Judiths facing contemporary Goliaths and Holifernes. They have acted out of their faith convictions, which move them to act not just for themselves but for the well-being of the planet, their neighbors—the entire human and biotic community.

In a similar way, religious men and women around the country have been developing new models of care for the earth, such as the use of their congregational lands for the development of land trusts, community gardens, and new farm initiatives, i.e., community-supported agriculture, food processing facilities, orchards, forests, and the restoration of lakes. These communal witnesses to earth awareness demonstrate a vital new trajectory in the experience of those wedding liturgy and justice. Some congregations have even moved their institutions to total reliance on locally produced food and have created ecological habitats for their own community lives.

Justice in the contemporary world must include an ecological and social awareness. Love of God, love of the earth, and love of the poor more fully incarnate the Mystical Body's self-awareness. Solidarity necessarily involves the biosphere; hence, the integrity of creation is part of contemporary Catholic Social Teaching.

John Paul II takes table fellowship to be the root metaphor for the Catholic understanding of justice. He argues for "each people's right to be seated at the table of the common banquet."[10] John Paul interprets the lack of North-South collaboration in development as re-enacting the indifference of the rich man to Lazarus. The poor, the Holy Father argues, are neighbors and helpers, "to be made sharers, on a par with ourselves, in the banquet of life to which all are equally called by God."[11] Human history, for the Pope, "is not a straightforward process, as it were, automatic and in itself limitless."[12]

The intent of liturgy is to transform the world into a mirror of itself, a banquet of self-sacrificing love. Think about your family and the table rules. Is everyone called to the table? Is everyone's presence expected? What common courtesies are expected at your table? Do you express gratitude for what you

[10] *Sollicitundino Rei Socialis* (On Social Concern, 1987) 32.
[11] Ibid., 32.
[12] Ibid., 27.

have? Do you remember the many hands involved in bringing food to your table: the hand of God, the hands of farmers, transporters, processors, grocers, and preparers? How is food distributed and shared at your table? Are you expected to try a bit of everything? What is your family's attitude toward wasting food, toward overeating? Is special consideration given to sick members of the family, to guests? Do you take care to recycle bottles and other food containers? Do you compost? Do you say to yourself and to family members, "Be polite, be considerate, be unselfish, don't talk with your mouth full, eat it, it's good for you?" Where did all of this come from?

Think about your community's table—where the community's work gets done. Think about the habitat of your community, the environmental, social, economic, political life of your community—the table wider than your family table. What is the greatest injustice in the local community? How are the poor treated? The earth? Those in need? What rules ought to be enacted to counter injustices? What can be done to enforce these rules? The aim of politics is the realization of justice and peace. Politics is the art of seeking and fostering the common good. Politics is what establishes the rules whereby people work, compete, raise families, and share the benefits and burdens of society. These rules are either just or unjust. The goods and services available or needed in the community are like the food present or lacking on a family's table. Public policy helps or hinders people as they present themselves at the common table and seek their just share of the table fare. How is the common good identified and protected? And so we say: "Money talks. What goes around, comes around. It's not right! Special interests have too much power. They never listen to us." Think about the table of the Lord.

Who is called to the Lord's table? Does Christ have any expectations of his disciples when they gather at his table? How are disciples expected to treat one another? Consider the actions at the table of the Lord: assembling, singing, hungering for the word, listening, expressing gratitude and wonder, blessing bread, breaking bread, sharing bread, eating bread, drinking the fruit of the vine, remembering the example we have been given, and being sent into the world to transform it.

We repeat to others: "Love your neighbors as yourself. Remember, as long as you did it to one of these, the little ones, you did it to me. Blessed are the peacemakers, for they shall see God. Do unto others as I have done to you. This is my body, this is my blood. Take and eat."

Our table fellowship reminds us that we are created in God's image to be sons and daughters of God, brothers and sisters to one another in Christ and temples of the Holy Spirit. We are members of the Mystical Body. We become conscious of this as we live and think and move and have our being. We have personal dignity. We are called to participate in community to seek the common good. The goods of creation are meant for all, so that all might flourish. We are called to be good and just stewards of creation, and lovers of the earth, in its origin and destiny. Through our work, we are called to continuing participation in God's creation. Those who are weak, sick, or poor are entitled to particular attention.

Think about your tables—family tables, community tables, faith tables. Who eats? How is food prepared? How is it shared? And who gets to talk? What do they say? Tables are for eating and tables are for talking. Eating is a moral act. We shape each other and our world at our tables. Our choices create our tables, our food, our talk.

The stories of the people of God are often stories of land, people, and food. Consider the Genesis story of Adam and Eve. They were given the responsibility to tend the garden and to keep it. They were given the responsibility to care for all of creation. Evil's entry into the world is described in the Scriptures as a decision to eat the fruit of the tree of the knowledge of good and evil. Responsibility and choice were associated with the act of eating. Similarly, when Jesus had to choose to accept or reject the direction that his Father had chosen for him, that choice was identified by the drinking of a cup: "Take this cup away from me" (Luke 22:42).[13] This was the voice of Jesus. Eating and responsible decision-making are thus conjoined in the life of Jesus. Eating becomes a symbol of deciding,

[13] Scriptural citations are taken from the NAB.

of responsible decision making. As eating can symbolize responsible choice, so too can eating demonstrate moral behavior. Eating is a moral act.

Eating is significant not only to personal behavior and individual actions; it is also related to a social order, to a food system. Consider the story of Joseph at the end of Genesis. At first, this story is one of fraternal conflict and jealousy, when Joseph's brothers sell him into slavery in Egypt. However, while in Egypt, Joseph demonstrates his managerial expertise, gets noticed by the Pharaoh, and is put in charge of Pharaoh's food policy. Joseph takes the land of all who abide in Egypt in exchange for seed and food. People readily give up their freedom in order to eat. The social order becomes centralized in Pharaoh's hands, managed by Joseph. Out of hunger, people give themselves over to slavery. The social order in which slavery was acceptable as recompense for hunger becomes a way of life in Egypt: "Joseph told the people, 'Now that I have acquired you and your land for Pharaoh, here is your seed for sowing the land. . . . ' And the people answered, 'You have saved our lives! We are grateful to my lord that we can be Pharaoh's slaves" (Gen 47:23, 25). A food system can become a structure of unfreedom. In God's created world, where the Hebrews that they were created to "tend and keep the garden" and "stand erect," where Saint Paul says human beings are meant to "rise to full stature," we find structures of food production and consumption that are systems of unfreedom, of slavery.

Remember the table of the Lord and how he washed the feet of his disciples. Remember how he asked us to remember his action . . . of feeding us with his Body and Blood. Remember how his table fellowship included a lying friend's decisive act—Judas' momentous meal. Remember how Jesus treated with dignity and kindness, but nonetheless with decisiveness, those who condemned him: "It would have been better that he never have lived" (Matt 26:24). "Today you will be with me in paradise" (Luke 23:43). The meal of suffering is also the meal of justice and love, where we partake of the fruit of the vine and the work of human hands. Those who prepare holy food prepare it for a holy world, for the world's sanctification and redemption.

The NCRLC has a campaign directed at eaters, those who shape the structure of agriculture and the structure of our food system. By our choices we shape the world. The questions to be asked are, Do you purchase food from retailers who support family farmers? Do you eat food that was grown by farmers who treated their animals with dignity and respect, who raised the animals humanely? Does your food come from local farmers or does it travel a long distance to get to your table? Does your food contribute to global climate change? Is the food you eat part of a sustainable food system that contributes to the well being of unknown future generations, to a healthy environment, to a local community in a rural or urban area that has a great deal of vitality? Or will the food you eat come from a system that depopulates the countryside and demeans farmers, farm workers, food process workers, corporate executives and their families?

Eating is a moral act. We are what we eat! And we can ask ourselves who is at the table. What are they saying about the food system? Consider the powerful words of James Schmitmeyer, NCRLC member and rural pastor:

> The picture shows a close-up of a farmer's hands. His is wearing gloves. The hands are pressed together palm to palm and he holds them at waist level. You do not see the farmer's face. Only his hands. And wrapped around his gloved hands are strands of twisted barbed wire—like a rope—binding them like those of a prisoner or a slave. This photograph is part of a campaign of the National Catholic Rural Life Conference. It is an informational campaign meant to stimulate thinking about issues of justice in the production of our food and the people who labor to produce it. The campaign is called "Eating is a Moral Act," and it attempts to open our eyes to see what we otherwise ignore: To take notice of deficiencies of justice in the midst of mounting riches. To take note of the hard work of farming, the dangerous working of fishing, the tedious work of processing . . . all those raw and unsettling realities not reflected in the soft glow of the candlelight in fine restaurants; human realities blanched pale in the glaring convenience of fast food, economic oligopolies glossed over by plastic packaging by the handful of companies who control our eating at bargain prices and bargain basement wages. "Look, take a good hard look at what you are overlook-

ing!" This is the cry of all prophetic voices throughout the history of faith: to see what is otherwise ignored! Though it is difficult to admit, we all have this tendency to overlook essential elements of justice. Whether it is the food we eat or the clothes we wear or the services we use, we all have a tendency to take our comforts for granted. We set a fine table for our fine foods and our refined talk. And on the other side of this otherwise innocuous tendency comes the surprised reaction when we are confronted with words warning us about the long-term results of our lack of attention. This is our habit and it leads to sin, the sin of overlooking the wages paid, the pollution made, the plans laid by the rich, and those for whom the buck never stops.

My words carry a terrible sting and our reaction is certainly predictable. We quickly reach for some ointment to alleviate the pain caused by these accusations. Amidst the soft glow of candlelight at our dinner tables we begin reciting the soothing mantras of neo-liberal doctrine: "It's a global economy," we whisper to ourselves, "free markets benefit everyone." And the automatic ritual allows us to better ignore disturbing reports and pass over such facts that, since the passage of NAFTA, the working poor in Mexico has climbed from 40% to 60% of the population. We know many such changes. Here is another one: "The low wages of the maquiladores simply reflect the lower standard of living in that country." It's a comforting verse. It numbs the gnawing fact that the average wage of $5.00 a day in Ciudad Juarez, Mexico, must buy food that costs the same as across the river in El Paso, Texas. We ignore many things at home as well. We ignore the growing poverty in rural America. We are ignorant of the loss of 300,000 family farms in the last twenty years. See the wages withheld from people who work the land, says St. James' Gospel. Take a look at what you'd rather ignore!

But it's so distressing to be reminded of this, you say. It's so frustrating to be aware of injustice and not be able to do anything about it. Indeed, what is the purpose of this diatribe? What can sincere people do in a world where injustice exists and will always exist? Why bring up these unpleasant facts? These are valid protests. Religious rites, worship services, liturgies are to be banquets of joy and peace. Eating is a moral act, and sometimes a religious act. Yet, the gratitude for holy food and the salvation it brings is fully expressed only when we remember that unleavened bread was first eaten by slaves on the run and the cup of some drink is a cup of suffering. Just as I believe that Bread and Wine are transformed, so are we transformed . . . transformed into people of compassion, people who see what others overlook, people who can begin to trace the vague outlines of the prophetic vision of the Reign of God where justice and mercy embrace and a grand table is set. Where bankers sit next to farmers, border guards converse with the undocumented and ranchers share toasts with environmentalists. Where work gloves lie next to linen napkins, hands are scrubbed, feet are washed, thirst is quenched, hunger satisfied and there's no hint of justice, no whisper of enslavement . . . no sign of barbed wire anywhere![14]

Eating is a moral act. Our tables need to include those who have been excluded. Our talk needs to include our farmers and their families, the rural communities, our environment, our landscape, our countryside, and our religious and moral values. We are what we eat. By our choices we shape our world. By our conversations, our talking, our praying, our liturgy, our justice, we live the Body of Christ and shape the reign of God. Let us pray together to forge a world of justice, ecological harmony, and peace.

[14] James Schmitmeyer's reflection was written for the NCRLC's "Eating Is a Moral Act" campaign.

Zeni Fox

Church Leadership Today: Building Right Relationships

A new leadership scene has emerged in the Roman Catholic Church today. It has particular contours here in the United States, but our experience finds parallels in other countries and cultures. The new realities bring both opportunities and challenges to the community of the Church, which has as a central tenet a commitment to justice. This paper will first explore some of these new developments, noting their rootedness in the documents of the Second Vatican Council. It will then propose some actions that are needed, in light of these changes, to build right relationships, to bring forth a more just Church.

First, a context for our reflections. Today, much more than fifty years ago, there is a general awareness that the Church is always in a process of renewal. It is, after all, a human institution. The Body of Christ, certainly, with a Head who is divine, but members who are—well, us—imperfect, flawed, at times sinful. And, the Church is an institution within history, and therefore in a continual process of adaptation, guided by the Spirit to respond to the signs of the times. Yet at times, it is not responsive to those promptings. People sometimes respond to the Church's failures and imperfections with surprise, shock, unmitigated anger, whereas perhaps the kind of compassion Jesus showed for the failures of individuals is what is needed as a response to the institution.

Walter Wink places the constant task of renewal in a theological framework, which sheds light on institutional life. He posits that the New Testament "Powers" (see, for example, Eph 6:12) are the institutions, structures, and systems of our social reality, and not only the outer, visible dimensions of these structures, but also their inner spirituality or corporate culture or collective personality. In this sense one could speak of our institutions as having institutional souls, inner lives greater than their outward manifestations. Reflecting further on "the Powers," especially Colossians 1:16-17, Wink asserts that the "social structures of reality are creations of God . . . made to serve the humanizing purposes of God in the world." God upholds these structures in being, condemns them insofar as they are destructive of full human actualization and presses for their transformation into a more humane order. Therefore the Powers "must be honored, criticized, resisted and redeemed."[1] It is, indeed, an invitation to build right relationships within our institutions in a spirit of hope and confidence.

Vatican II: Key Themes

In reflecting on Vatican II in relation to our topic, five key themes will be explored. Each of these has influenced changes in Church leadership that we are experiencing today, and each requires a fuller structural embodiment in the life of the community. First, a brief review of the progress that has been made in implementing the vision of Vatican II is in order.

Full, Conscious and Active Participation in the Liturgy. This phrase appears fifteen times in the Constitution on the Sacred Liturgy; it was a call to a change from a passive to an active laity. The document reminds us that the liturgy is the summit and fount of the life of the Church; what we do at liturgy expresses and empowers the life of the community. Participation was named a right and obligation, flowing from baptism (SC 14). Laypersons may have a particular office to perform at liturgy (SC 28); servers, readers, commentators, and members

---

[1] Walter Wink, *Engaging the Powers* (Minneapolis: Fortress Press, 1992) 3–10, 65–66.

of the choir exercise a ministry (SC 29). A new vision. And in many ways this vision has brought significant change to the life of our communities. In many parishes we observe multiple ministers exercising diverse roles in the liturgy celebrations. We also observe a more involved assembly, actively sharing with word, gesture, and song in the celebration. This active participation is sign and symbol of the larger life of the Church, with the emergence of new roles of multiple persons engaged in multiple ministries.

Collegiality, Collaboration. It has been said that the exposition of the doctrine of the collegiality of the bishops with the pope, their sharing together in pastoral responsibility for the Church, is one of the primary definitions of Vatican II. While the concept properly refers to the pope and bishops, the idea of the laity's co-responsibility or collaboration in the work of the Church is similarly rooted in the concept of shared mission, of a body wherein members are in communion with one another. In the Dogmatic Constitution on the Church pastors are reminded that "it is their exalted office so to be shepherds of the faithful and also recognize the latter's contribution and charism that everyone in his own way will, with one mind, cooperate in the common task" (LG 30). Furthermore, the laity are called upon to contribute: "By reason of the knowledge, competence or pre-eminence which they have the laity are empowered—indeed sometimes obliged—to manifest their opinion on those things which pertain to the good of the Church" (LG 37). And not only should the advice of laity be sought but pastors should willingly "assign duties to them in the service of the Church, leaving them freedom and scope for acting" (LG 37).

Much progress has been made embodying this vision in the structures of Church life, including in canon law. John Beal, a canonist, has said: "The reforms that followed the council and have now been incorporated into the revised code opened wide the door for a variety of forms of participation by lay people in the Church's sanctifying and teaching missions." He notes that there has been the creation (or recovery) of consultative bodies, at the diocesan (Synod, finance council, pastoral council—to include "especially lay persons") and parish levels (finance and pastoral councils). In addition, other structures and processes not mentioned in the Code have developed: diocesan and parish school boards, advisory boards for health care, social service and educational institutions, and various kinds of structured consultation regarding such actions as the closure or merger of parishes and schools. Beal acknowledges that these bodies do not make the final decisions but observes, "Despite its reservation of most choice-making authority to bishops and pastors, the code evidences a strong preference for collaborative rather than unilateral decision-making."[2] As we try to embody the council's vision of co-responsibility in Church life, examination of what the code mandates, what it permits, and efforts toward beginning or strengthening needed structures is a concrete exercise in building right relationships.

In addition to a consultative role in decision-making, certain diocesan and parish leadership positions that entail some share in the function of governance are open to laypeople, including some which meet the canonical criteria for ecclesiastical offices, that is, "constituted in a stable manner by divine or ecclesiastical law to be exercised for a spiritual purpose" (*Code of Canon Law* 145 [1]). At the parish level this includes parish administrators, principals of parish schools, and directors of religious education. The bishop has broad discretion to share significant parts of his executive authority with lay people, by delegation, and in a subordinate and dependent way, thereby sharing governance power.[3] In other words, the emphasis on the active participation of the laity in the Church, in collabora-

---

[2] John Beal, "Lay People and Church Governance: Oxymoron or Opportunity," *Together in God's Service: Toward a Theology of Ecclesial Lay Ministry* (Washington, D.C.: USCC, 1998) 103–07. The Diocese of Oakland has instituted a new body, the Lay Ecclesial Ministers Council. Parallel to the presbyteral and diaconal councils, it is consultative to the bishop, inaugurated by him after consultation with the presbyteral council. Recognizing the importance of this initiative, the National Association for Lay Ministry gave the council its Spirit of the Conference Award in May 2001, noting that the council "is the first of its kind in the country where lay ecclesial ministers have been placed in an official consultative capacity to their bishop within the structure of the diocese."

[3] Ibid., 108–12, 120.

tion with the hierarchy, has indeed brought about new patterns of church governance: new bodies, new roles, new processes.

Using the Gifts of All the Baptized. The council affirmed a Church in which multiple gifts are present *and* called on leaders to use these gifts for the life and mission of the community. The Decree on the Apostolate of the Laity states: "For the exercise of the apostolate [the Holy Spirit] gives the faithful special gifts" (DAL 3). The action of the laity "is so necessary that without it the apostolate of the pastors will frequently be unable to obtain its full effect" (DAL 10). Much is written today about the decline in the number of priests and vowed religious. Recently the National Conference of Catholic Bishops examined the impact of fewer priests on pastoral ministry. Their executive summary gives some statistics which add an interesting perspective to our topic, and the question of "decline."

> There has been a 30+ percent increase in the number of lay ecclesial ministers over the past eight years. There are approximately 30,000 at this time. Another 30,000 are currently in formation in degree or certificate programs across the country. There are over 13,000 deacons in the United States, with another 2,500 in formation. There are approximately 12,000 youth ministers. There are approximately 150,000 Catholic school teachers.[4]

Not included in this overview is the vast number of volunteers engaged in many aspects of ministry, and the many professionals working in settings beyond the parish.

The preparation for these new ministers has had significant attention in the Church in the United States. It is worth remembering the kinds of programs of preparation for ministry available before the council. Priests were prepared in seminaries, vowed religious within their communities and sometimes their colleges. One graduate school of theology was open to other

---

[4] "The Study of the Impact of Fewer Priests on the Pastoral Ministry," prepared for the Spring General Meeting of the National Conference of Catholic Bishops, June 15–17, 2000, by the Committees on Priestly Life and Ministry, African American Catholics, the Diaconate, Hispanic Affairs, Home Missions, Pastoral Practices, Vocations, and the Sub-Committee on Lay Ecclesial Ministry, unpublished, iv–v.

than those preparing for ordination. The Confraternity of Christian Doctrine provided preparation programs for catechists and other roles such as the fishers; these programs were of a relatively brief duration. After the council, dioceses, colleges, universities, seminaries and even independent groups initiated programs to prepare laity for active roles in ministry.

Today one sees signs of increasingly more focused attention on and more diverse efforts in ministry formation. A quick assessment includes the following examples. Guidelines for diaconal formation have been published by the Bishops' Conference. In addition to general programs of ministry formation, most dioceses offer many programs preparing people for specific roles, including catechists, lectors, eucharistic ministers, leaders of bereavement and Bible study groups, and others. This spring, the National Association for Lay Ministry planned a pre-conference on the formation of laity for ministry, anticipating thirty to fifty participants; one hundred and twenty attended. The Sub-Committee on Lay Ministry recently disseminated a Center for Applied Research in the Apostolate (CARA) study on the spiritual formation of lay ecclesial ministers.

One can interpret these developments as a flourishing of the gifts of great numbers of the baptized, a diversification of ministries, an increase in those called to labor in the vineyard. The official Church has taken a significant role in these initiatives, and individual members have responded generously to the call to ministry. Especially notable is the pastoral letter by Cardinal Roger Mahony and the priests of the Archdiocese of Los Angeles, which describes the flourishing of this diversity of ministries in parishes today and calls for the collaboration of all the baptized in the work of the Church.[5]

Laity Employed in the Church. While certainly not a strong theme at the Second Vatican Council, in light of current developments it is worth noting that already with the Decree on the Apostolate of the Laity there was recognition of this mode of

[5] Mahony, Cardinal Roger and the Priests of the Archdiocese of Los Angeles. *As I Have Done For You: A Pastoral Letter on Ministry* (Chicago: Liturgy Training Publications, 2000).

service in the Church. The text offers both affirmation and challenge:

> Worthy of special respect and praise in the Church are the laity, single or married, who, in a definitive way or for a period, put their person and their professional competence at the service of institutions and their activities. . . . Pastors are to welcome these lay persons with joy and gratitude. They will see to it that their condition of life satisfies as perfectly as possible the requirements of justice, equity and charity. . . . They should too be provided with the necessary training and with spiritual comfort and encouragement (DAL 22).

In this document, the ministry of these laity is not given a name. In the United States, the Bishops' Conference has been pondering this new reality; in their most recent statement they use the title "lay ecclesial ministers." The bishops offer a strong affirmation of the role and work of these ministers and catalogue the multiple questions which need to be addressed in order to adapt more adequately the structures of Church life,[6] so as to give them "necessary training and . . . spiritual comfort and encouragement."

Areas of Concern

Our review of some themes from Vatican II outlines the continuity between the vision of the documents and developments in the Church today. However, relative to each theme, we as Church still have significant work to do to embody the vision more adequately.

Multicultural Riches, Scarcity. Every study done of the Church in the United States documents that we are growing more multicultural, increasing in diversity. Certainly, there is a widespread understanding of the richness that diverse cultural gifts bring to the community, as publications, workshops, conferences, and celebrations attest. However, studies of the formal

---

[6] *Lay Ecclesial Ministry: The State of the Questions: A Report of the Subcommittee on Lay Ministry* (Washington, D.C.: USCC, 1999).

ministers in the Church—priests, lay ecclesial ministers, deacons—show that Native Americans, Hispanic/Latino Americans, and Asian/Pacific Americans are significantly underrepresented in these leadership roles. The question of how to call forth and prepare ministers from these communities is a complex one. In part, it requires an adaptation of expectations and structures. For example, often dioceses have a master's degree as a requirement for positions held by lay ecclesial ministers. This excludes many in these communities, even those already exercising leadership, from being credentialed for such positions, because they do not have the requisite bachelor's degree. Furthermore, preparation programs are often monocultural, lacking the kinds of signs, symbols, rituals, interpersonal relationships, and assignments that invite persons of diverse cultures into participation, affirming the value of the particular gifts different groups bring to the community. And parishes often lack the mechanisms for identifying the leaders and potential leaders in minority communities, and calling them into ministry.

Obstacles to Collaboration. Anecdotal evidence and the many books, articles, and workshops on the topic of collaboration demonstrate that the vision of a co-responsible Church is not yet fulfilled. Certainly this is understandable when we review the conflicting expectations that arise from two ecclesiologies, each present in the Church today, one emphasizing hierarchical, authoritarian models and the other communion models. Even if this were not so, behaviorists remind us that we are much more influenced by behaviors that have been modeled to us than by ideas. Therefore, the behaviors of a Church that expected laity to be passive and obedient still affects laity and clergy alike in diverse ways. Beal observes: "The principle of communion can be violated equally by management styles that eschew consultation or treat it as an empty formality for reaching a foreordained conclusion and by attitudes that reduce having a meaningful voice in decisions to having a deliberative vote."[7] Compounding the difficulty is the fact that secular research demonstrates that managers consistently see

[7] Beal, 107.

themselves as more collaborative than do their employees,[8] helping to demonstrate the complexity of the human interrelationships involved in these efforts. Precisely because we are human persons collaboration, working together, will always require effort, and renewed effort. But because of our theological and experiential legacy, at the moment our rhetoric is more advanced than our practice, and ongoing attention to the theological base for and mechanisms of collaboration is essential for building right relationships.

Just Treatment of Church Workers. Too often when people think of this topic they focus simply on issues of salary and benefits. It is much broader and must be grounded in a more adequate theology. Yves Congar has stressed that in reflecting on ministry, the plural noun is essential, that in addition to presbyteral ministry there is also "a multitude of diverse modes of service, more or less stable or occasional, more or less spontaneous or recognized and when the occasion arises consecrated." He observes that while these ministries have indeed existed, they were not called by their true name, nor were their place and status in ecclesiology recognized. He concludes: "To move on to this . . . recognition is extremely important for any just vision of things."[9] Progress has been made in recent years on a fuller understanding of ministry and ministries, but as the subtitle of the recent document of the bishops on lay ecclesial ministry demonstrates, to date they can only name "the state of the questions."

Of course, there is a practical dimension to this question as well. The organization giving ongoing reflection and guidance in this area is The National Association of Church Personnel Administrators (NACPA). NACPA's efforts include first of all a vision, rooted in Catholic social justice principles, presented in two seminal documents. Here they address issues of work and

---

[8] For a fuller treatment of this topic, with bibliographic references, see Zeni Fox, "Preparing for Collaborative Ministry," *Theology of Priesthood and Seminary Formation* (Washington, D.C.: National Catholic Educational Association, 1989).

[9] Yves Congar, "My Path-Findings in the Theology of Laity and Ministries," *The Jurist* 32 (1972) 169–88.

justice, which are applicable to all church workers, bishops and volunteers, parish and diocesan personnel.[10] In addition, they offer practical guidance through publications and consultations on a broad range of relevant topics, including such things as participation in decision making, affirmative action, performance appraisal and compensation systems, and grievance procedures. The vision of comprehensive policies, inclusive of priests, vowed religious, and laypersons which NACPA advocates, is very unevenly embodied in dioceses and represents a rigorous agenda for building right relationships.

Employees? Ministers? Lay ecclesial ministers have reported that at times some rather dismissively say their ministry is a job; they are paid to do it. Interestingly, people do not say this about priests or vowed religious. Furthermore, in our tradition, a priest makes a permanent commitment to his diocese (or order), and enters into a reciprocal relationship that is not at all easily sundered. A lay ecclesial minister may view his or her commitment to Church ministry as permanent, but there is no way that this commitment can be made public, nor is there a mutuality of relationship. When the U.S. Bishops' Subcommittee on Lay Ministry held consultations with lay ecclesial ministers, the members were struck by the language of call and commitment—the language of vocation. They struggled with the implications of this and acknowledged that the entire Church must nurture and discern all vocations to ministry. But mechanisms for this have not yet been developed, although a few dioceses have begun to address the issue.

As Roman Catholics, ritual plays an important part in our life, our imagination. Questions of right relationship arise in this regard; these can be framed most simply with a quick contrast. Men preparing for priesthood move through a series of ritual steps: installation as acolyte, as lector; ordination as deacon, as priest. Ordinations are the occasions of great celebrations, with many persons participating; the ritual is elaborate,

---

[10] *The Individual and the Institution: Strengthening Working Relationships in the Church* and "Workplace Justice: Guidance for Church Leaders" (Cincinnati: National Association of Church Personnel Administrators, 1994 and 2000, respectively).

solemn, filled with meaning. On the other hand, there is no official ritual marking the beginning of the ministry of lay ecclesial ministers. Their new relationship with the community is not symbolically represented and celebrated.[11]

An added dimension of this question has to do with the relationship of the lay ecclesial minister and the bishop. At the present time, lay ecclesial ministers in parishes are hired by pastors, with no official reference to the bishop, who is the pastoral leader of the diocese and "the visible source and foundation" of its unity (LG 23). This anomaly is addressed by Bishop Clark, who says that when "the Subcommittee on Lay Ministry politely concluded that 'the relationship of the bishop to the lay ecclesial minister needs further attention and clarification' . . . the committee has almost certainly understated the enormous theological and practical problems with which we now grapple." Placing his reflections in the context of an understanding of Church as communion-mission, Clark advocates for a more developed theology, a better structural framework for communion, and a spirituality of communion which truly values the gifts of all.[12] Truly an agenda for building right relationships.

A Just Church: Leaven for a Just Society

One of the great mandates of the council, one frequently stressed by Pope John Paul II, is the call to the Church to strive to transform the social order, to evangelize the culture by bringing Gospel values to bear on the society. One way to do this is by being a model of justice in our relationships within the Church, by being a testing ground and training place for those principles and practices that embody right relationships. Our theology powerfully articulates the dignity of each Christian,

---

[11] John Grondelski has a helpful article on this topic: "Lay Ministries? A Quarter Century of *Ministeria Quaedam,*" *The Irish Theological Quarterly* 63 (1998) 272–82. See also my own *New Ecclesial Ministry: Lay Professionals Serving the Church* (Kansas City, Mo.: Sheed and Ward, 1997) ch. 16.

[12] Bishop Matthew Clark, "The Relationship of the Bishop and Lay Ecclesial Minister," *Origins* (April 5, 2001) 676–81. See also Fox, ch. 16.

each a priest, prophet, king, and invites each to participation in the mission of the Church. The emergence of multiple ministries and ministers marks an important step in living this vision, but the fuller incorporation into ideology, structures, and attitudes remains a task before us.

Our theology also affirms the primacy of the individual, made in the image of God, yet always in communion with others. Again, the invitation is to right relationships, relationships which foster the development of each church minister, the participation of all members of the community, and just practices. Certainly, work toward these ends, from the development of ministry formation programs to that of policies and procedures for employment and compensation is in progress, but more is still needed.

Finally, in any consideration of issues which call for a greater attention to matters of justice, it is well to recall that always the command of love is the informing principle, not only as a goal —to create a more loving community—but also as a means—to do so always with love. By living this, the Church will be the leaven it is called to be and will work powerfully to transform the culture.

Frances B. O'Connor, C.S.C.

The Injustice of the Lack of Justice for Women in Liturgy

For years I sat in the pews unaware of how the exclusion of women from full participation in liturgy impacted their lives. Then, in the early 1990s it was reported that many Catholic bishops of the world claimed it was only North American women who were dissatisfied with their place in the Church. My concern about these reports and my international experiences prompted me to undertake a study, asking women how they felt about their role in the Church and liturgy. I interviewed women in Asia, Africa, Latin America, and the U.S. and as indicated in my book, *Like Bread Their Voices Rise: Global Women Challenge the Church*,[1] I found that women around the world want to be more involved in the liturgy.

My research revealed two predominant reasons for women's discontent, which were consistent on every continent: one, women's desire to serve their people, particularly in ways they were not being well served by their priests; and two, women's exclusion from decisions affecting their lives in the Church and liturgy. These two reasons exemplify the lack of justice for women in the Church's liturgy.

---

[1] Notre Dame, Ind.: Ave Maria Press, 1993.

87

Power and position were not women's motivation; service and a desire for inclusion and representation were. Women in the United States felt most called to administering the sacraments of the sick, baptism and reconciliation, and to preaching on the Word of God. The sacraments noted require a special presence at times of birth, death, and sickness of both soul and body. The need to respond to such moments in the lives of the people of God is equally as strong as the need to break open the Word of God and share it from a woman's perspective. As recently as June 1, 2001, a news brief item in the *National Catholic Reporter (NCR)* noted the unavailability of priests to administer the sacrament of the sick in hospitals in the U.S. Both female and male pastoral care chaplains are present, but they are officially prevented from performing this much needed service.

Women from developing countries spoke with me about visiting the sick in their rural parishes and being unable to administer the last sacraments or bring Communion. They expressed their desire to respond to the needs of their people. Frequently, by the time they would walk back to the parish to get a priest, the sick person had died. Others spoke of their desire to preach, to break open the Word from a woman's perspective, and to hear a homily that would touch their souls. Still others maintained that the Church does not treat women as Jesus would, because it only considers them for those roles or services that priests or laymen do not want to do.

I also learned that in many countries where, even under the present guidelines, more opportunities for service could be given to women, bishops and priests still do not allow them to serve as lectors or eucharistic ministers, take Communion to the sick, be altar servers, or even study theology. These are further examples of the lack of justice for women.

The second recurring issue women identified was that of exclusion. In the U.S., where women perform many ministries, the critical issue is not ordination but rather, the patriarchal structure of the institutional Church. As Maria Riley notes, "The central issue is exclusion. Women are excluded from effective power in helping to shape the church's mission, its teaching, its laws, and its liturgy. Only after decisions are made, are women granted their 'appropriate role.' Women do not even have a voice in defining what is appropriate for them."[2] It is not difficult to recognize the injustice of having to adhere to laws and regulations that women have no voice in making. Bishop P. Francis Murphy, in an article in *Commonweal* in 1992, expressed it well. He quoted the Pope as saying, "Rule by man over woman, is not part of God's plan." Murphy went on to say:

> In fact, dominance pervades our church, a dominance that excludes the presence, the insights, and experience of women from the table where the formulation of the church's doctrine takes place and the exercise of its power is discerned. It likewise excludes women from presiding at the table where the community of faith is fed. This patriarchy continues to permeate the church and supports a climate that not only robs women of their full personhood, but also encourages men to be domineering, aggressive and selfish.[3]

Strong words from a bishop and defender of women's rights, who unfortunately died of cancer in 1999.

Women from countries other than the U.S. expressed the same concerns. Women religious in South India, for instance, wrote a letter to Pope John Paul II, challenging his letter that denied women the right to priesthood and called it "God's Will." These women responded, not because this is the most crucial of women's issues, but because the Church's adamant patriarchal position excludes women from any major leadership or decision-making role within the Church. Hence, the real issues at stake are the fundamental rights of women as baptized persons, and their equal membership and inclusion in the Church. A woman theologian from India wrote eloquently about the problem of exclusion:

> I wish the women in the Catholic Church would form a union and stage a walk-out. . . . I am tired of a worship that fails to recognize my existence. . . . To be a woman in the church means to be invisible. . . . We have no say in the formulation of

[2] Maria Riley, *In God's Image* (Kansas City, Mo.: Sheed & Ward, 1995) 8.
[3] P. Francis Murphy, "Let's Start Over," *Commonweal* (September 1992) 11–15.

Canon Law . . . our spirituality does not shape doctrine. And
theology based on our God-experience is dismissed as "feminist
nonsense."[4]

From Uganda, East Africa, Sister Anna Mary Mukamuwezi
wrote in an article entitled "Church Moral Teaching and the
Dignity of an African Woman":

I believe women are asking the church to examine itself in relation to women, the attitudes of the clergy and hierarchy towards women . . . the exclusion of women from preaching to
the whole people of God. . . . Because women are excluded at
the heart of the church, the church itself lacks a fullness of
human reflection, male and female, in the formation of its doc-
trinal, moral and pastoral life.[5] (A major part of the Church's
pastoral life is its liturgy).

What can women around the world teach liturgists about
injustice in the Catholic Church? The most obvious answer is
first and foremost that this is not just a North American concern but a global concern.

In regard to the issue of exclusion, one response of liturgists
ought to be to work toward eliminating all sexist, non-inclusive
language from readings, documents, and hymns. As Catholics,
we have the right to expect that our prayers and hymns are
inclusive of both women and men and that symbols and im-
agery of God not be exclusively masculine. "Our language,"
notes scripture scholar Barbara Reid, "must not perpetuate the
attitude that man is the paradigm and that woman is 'other.'
Thus, the language used both in addressing the assembly and
in referring to believers must express the reality that both
women and men are created in God's image."[6]

[4] Flavia D'Souza, "Women Live Their Faith in a Sexist Church," *Jeevad-
hara, A Journal of Christian Interpretation* (May 1990) 187.
[5] Sister Anna Mary Mukamuwezi, "Church Moral Teaching and the
Dignity of an African Woman," *Social Justice Newsletter* (August 1991) 11.
[6] Barbara Reid, "Liturgy, Scripture, and the Challenge of Feminism,"
Living No Longer for Ourselves, ed. Kathleen Hughes and Mark R. Francis
(Collegeville: The Liturgical Press, 1991) 134.

Yet another response of liturgists should be that women must be included in all ministries whenever possible. This includes preaching, even if for now it has to be after Communion. Conditioning congregations to see and hear women preach is preparation for women's full participation in ministry in the future.

Barbara Reid places a large part of the responsibility for inclusiveness on the shoulders of the liturgists when she says, "The language and symbols we use in our readings, preaching, hymns, and prayers, as well as the assignation of ministerial roles, reveal clearly our concepts of God, self and others." Then she asks, "Does the assigning of liturgical roles bespeak a theology that regards all the baptized as holy?" She answers her own question with a challenge: "The way we celebrate at the liturgical table is probably the best litmus test for the degree to which we are really committed to eliminating sexism from our midst. The language, symbols, and distribution of roles in the liturgical assembly must express that we are a church of equal disciples."[7]

Kathleen Hughes says, "Our worship, to be a worship of God in Spirit and in Truth, must be a concrete expression of right relationships, or it is worthless. It is an abomination."[8] When we exclude women, in whatever manner from our worship, it does not speak to right relationships; therefore, it is an abomination.

Nathan Mitchell underscores the importance of symbols appealing to our senses, saying that, "the seeing is in the listening, and the listening is in the seeing."[9] If in the listening, women do not hear the feminine referred to, they see only a liturgy for males. And if in the seeing, women perceive that males continue to dominate the liturgy with a few token females, women will not hear the message of equality the Church

[7] Ibid., 135–36.

[8] Kathleen Hughes, "Liturgy and Justice: An Intrinsic Relationship," *Living No Longer for Ourselves*, 41.

[9] Nathan Mitchell, "Seeing Salvation: Story, Rite and Word in the Easter Triduum," presentation given at Saint Mary's College, Notre Dame, Indiana, 2001.

preaches. The listening and the seeing must convey the same message. Liturgical actions and words must both speak to inclusion.

Why then the disparity between the Church's dialogue on justice and its ability to act? I believe the answer lies in the Church's understanding of the terms justice and equality, which in many instances differs substantially from the understanding some people might hold. But first, recall the inspiring words of the Synod of Bishops in 1971: "The church is bound to give witness to justice. She recognizes that everyone who ventures to speak to people about justice, must first be just in their own eyes."[10]

The Church must give witness to justice. The dilemma is that the institutional Church does not see the exclusion of women from the liturgy as an act of injustice, but rather as a matter of tradition. In contrast, many women and men, including some priests and bishops, see this exclusion as an act of injustice.

When some members of the Catholic hierarchy speak of men and women being created equal, they are speaking from a patriarchal worldview that sees men and women as complementary, with men always in the dominant role and women in the subservient role—together they complement each other.

When feminists speak of men and women being equal, they are speaking from the egalitarian worldview that sees them as truly equal. We use the same words, but we understand them differently—hence, the frequent confusion and misunderstandings. However, in the Pastoral Constitution on the Church in the Modern World, the Second Vatican Council was very explicit on this topic:

> All men and women are endowed with a rational soul and are created in God's image; they have the same nature and origin and, being redeemed by Christ, they enjoy the same divine calling and destiny; there is here a basic equality between all and it must be accorded ever greater recognition. . . . [Any] kind of

---

[10] David J. O'Brien and Thomas A. Shanon, eds., "Justice in the World," *Renewing the Earth: Catholic Documents on Peace, Justice and Liberation* (Garden City, N.Y.: Image Books, 1977) 400.

social or cultural discrimination in basic personal rights on the grounds of sex, race, color, social conditions, language or religion, must be curbed and eradicated as incompatible with God's design (GS 29).

It seems that since Vatican II, popes and bishops also interpret the word "discrimination" differently, as evidenced by the fact that women continue to be discriminated against by exclusion simply because they are women.

Bishop Francis Murphy believed women's equality to be as important as the issue Paul raised with Peter, namely, the admission of Gentiles into Christianity. Women's callings, as well as men's, should be tested. Justice demands it. The pastoral needs of the Church require it.[11]

The dilemma we are encountering is two very different understandings of equality, and consequently, two very different understandings of justice. Until there is true dialogue to reach a common understanding of these key terms, the institutional Church will not act justly toward women, nor accept them as truly equal human beings.

A specific example of the lack of justice and equality for women is the Vatican's insistence on continuing to address God in male terms only. In 1973 theologian Mary Daly offered a startling observation, "If God is male, then the male is God."[12] It appears the patriarchal dimension of the Church has ignored Daly's revelation because, still today, there are priests who are disciplined for using feminine language when referring to God. The seeing is in the listening! What women hear is what we see! And in liturgy, we see and hear of a male God only.

Michael Crosby, in his book *The Dysfunctional Church*, relates an example of the obsession of the curial leaders with preserving a male, patriarchal God:

> When in an address to 900,000 people in 1978, Pope John Paul I referred to God as a father, but even more a mother, no mention

---

[11] Murphy, "Let's Start Over," 14.

[12] Mary Daly, *Beyond God the Father* (Boston: Beacon Press, 1973) 19.

of the feminine idea of God was included in the official paper of the institutional church, *L'Osservatore Romano*. The Vatican printed the speech on September 21, 1978, but the references to God as female were censored."[13]

The disparity between the Church's dialogue on justice and its ability to act is obvious. Clearly, the two cannot and should not be separated.

Kathleen Hughes points out that there is an intrinsic relationship between cult and conduct, that worship is an expression of, and not a substitute for, social responsibility.[14] Liturgists have unique opportunities to help bring dialogue and justice into harmony in many ways. To ignore those opportunities for whatever reason contributes to patriarchal dominance in the Church. Therefore, liturgists should:

- Encourage priests to preach about women when women's stories arise in the Scriptures. Many priests avoid doing so because they really don't know what to say. A few hints from a friendly liturgist would help.

- Suggest that competent laywomen be given the opportunity to preach on appropriate occasions, if not after the gospel, then after Communion.

- Check the readings for sexist language and suggest substituting male references to God with "God," "Abba," or "Yahweh." It is not a complete answer, but a beginning.

- Indicate that offensive texts, such as "women be subject to your husbands," be either omitted or preached on in such a way so as to indicate their cultural context.

- Be sure that the hymns chosen have been checked for sexist language. There is nothing worse for women than having to sing about "sons of God" with no mention of God's daughters.

[13] Michael Crosby, *The Dysfunctional Church* (Notre Dame, Ind.: Ave Maria Press, 1991) 132.

[14] Hughes, 41.

These suggestions are all possible under the present norms. To some they may seem inconsequential, but they serve to raise the awareness of priests and other members of the assembly who are not yet sensitive to the fact that "the seeing is in the listening and the listening is in the seeing." Liturgists have the opportunity to emulate Jesus; not to do so is contributing to injustice. In this context, what are the beacons of light and hope for women at this time in the liturgy and the Church?

I believe that the brightest beacon of light and hope is the progress women have made since Vatican II. This is a relatively short time in the history of the Church, a Church that does not change rapidly. The traditional role of women in the early 1960s was to pray, pay, and obey, clean the church, arrange the flowers, and launder altar linens. The roles accessible to women today are those of lector, eucharistic minister, altar server, liturgist, members of parish councils, pastoral associates, retreat directors, Scripture scholars, and theologians.

At great risk and frequently at even greater price, women scholars opened the eyes and hearts of the people of God to the message of Jesus for women. They have revealed women's role in the early Church, told women's stories through the eyes of women, uncovered contributions of women hidden since the early centuries of Christianity, and disclosed the injustices of a patriarchal Church. Women, who comprise over 80 percent of parish ministers, have feminized the pastoral face of the Church, and with the help of liturgists will feminize the sacramental face of the Church, as well. But it will take time and courage. I do not mean to suggest we just sit back and wait for changes to occur. Rather, the changes we experience are the result of women and men's continual struggle for equality, one that becomes increasingly difficult as we come closer to achieving the goal of an egalitarian Church.

Other beacons of hope are the many feminist theologians, such as Elizabeth Johnson and Elizabeth Schüssler Fiorenza, who continue to contribute to a new understanding, a new way of acting and praying for women and men in today's Church.

Prophetic women such as Teresa Kane and the sisters of South India who spoke up even to the Pope about women's inequality in the Church, and Joan Chittister, who has written and lectured on women's inequality for thirty years in the face of hierarchical criticism, are examples for us.

Another beacon is John Wijngaards, former vicar general of the Mill Hill Missionaries and currently director of Housetop International Centre for Faith formation in London, who stated in an article entitled "My Stand for Women Priests" that "the official justification for banning women from the priesthood rests on the scaffolding of social prejudice and irrational practice."[15]

Msgr. Jack Egan, Chicago's social justice advocate, in a last testament that he sent to the *NCR* just days before his recent death, called for the ordination of women and for married priests:

> Even if there were no shortage of priests, even if we had an overabundance of quality male priests, the Catholic Church would still be required to rethink its exclusion of women from Holy Orders. It's not just a question of using women to fill in during an emergency. It is a matter, I believe, of social justice that all Catholics must come to terms with.[16]

These women and clerics certainly show courage, honesty, and a desire to close the gap between what the Church preaches about justice and how it acts. Such honesty demands a price, but we must remember Jesus paid with his life for the same kind of honesty. Can we do less?

Such examples may seem far removed from ordinary women and men, but there are also beacons of light and hope among us in our parishes. These are the strong leaders who are liturgists and who have the courage to take chances, to challenge and criticize in a constructive way the priests and people they work with, to be models who integrate justice into the liturgy so that "the seeing is in the listening and the listening is in the seeing." Other bright points of light that give us hope are:

---

[15] John Wijngaards, "My Stand for Women Priests," *New Women, New Church* (Spring 2000) 3.

[16] John J. Egan, "Use the Gifts God Gives," *NCR* (June 1, 2001) 7.

- homilists who use every opportunity to include women's issues or women's stories when they speak;

- women who own their own culpability in and submission to a patriarchal system that oppresses us;

- men and women, lay and clergy, who acknowledge the "elephant in the living room" and cease to pretend that all is well because "women have come a long way."

There are indeed signs of hope, but many see them as too few and too slow. Thomas Reese, editor of *America* magazine, asks the question:

> How does a reformer, then, respond to a period when reforms are coming slowly, if at all? I am afraid that the only answer is: with hard work, patience and love. . . . We have come to recognize in recent years the impossibility of creating political or economic utopias. We have come to realize that we cannot solve every problem faced by our children and our families. We cannot even reform ourselves to be the people we aspire to be. But that does not mean we stop trying.[17]

Liturgists need to develop a just and holy anger. Thomas Aquinas said it is morally wrong not to be angry when you encounter a situation of injustice. What is more unjust than to deprive women of full participation in the liturgy?

Like the disciples of Jesus in responding to the Canaanite woman, some in the Church want women to go away because women are troubling them. But today's Catholic women will not go away. They ground their hope in God's promises. The same assurance God gave to Moses that the people of Israel would be freed from the Egyptians can be given to women today. In Exodus 3:7-8 (NAB) we could read:

> God said, I have witnessed the affliction of my people in Egypt [women in the Church] and have heard their cry of complaint against their slave drivers so I know well what they are suffering. Therefore I have come down to rescue them from the hands

[17] Thomas Reese, "2001 and Beyond," *America* (June 21, 1997) 18.

of the Egyptians [patriarchy] and lead them out of that land into a good and spacious land flowing with milk and honey [the land of co-discipleship].

We cannot give up hope in the face of such a promise. We are all bound to suffer for our hopes, especially when their fulfillment seems so distant at times. Our unfulfilled hopes can often be very frustrating and can lead us into fear and anxiety. However, they also provide us with one of the most glorious of all opportunities—to hand on to the next generation of liturgists a movement filled with the promise of an egalitarian Church.

Daniel Lizárraga

Justice and Prayer in
Latino Communities in the United States

I am neither a liturgist nor a theologian. My remarks are not about liturgy per se; rather, they are about religious, cultural, and social issues that pertain to the Latino community in the United States. Of course, these issues cannot be separated from the Church's liturgical celebrations; therefore, my comments are directed to those involved in planning parish liturgies and in particular, to those in predominantly Anglo parishes that have experienced a recent influx of Latinos.

Before I address the issues concerning the Latino community, I want to note that my cultural experience as a Mexican American informs my remarks. At the same time, it is important to be mindful of the fact that in addition to Mexican Americans, the Latino community includes a number of different national communities—i.e., Puerto Ricans, Cuban Americans, Central and South Americans. Each of these communities has its own unique traditions and characteristics. They also share a number of things in common, including language, culture, and for the most part, religious beliefs.

I intend for the discussion that follows to encourage dialogue on matters pertaining to the Latino experience in the U.S. and to provide a basis for exchange on particular issues. Such an exchange may assist liturgists with their understanding of Latino culture and consequently, also assist them with providing for the initiation, development, and/or enhancement of prayer and liturgy at the local level.

Who is the Latino Community?

For me, one of the richest experiences of faith and culture was my involvement in the planning of *Encuentro 2000: Many Faces in God's House*. *Encuentro 2000* was the national jubilee event of the U.S. Church that took place in Los Angeles in July 2000. This gathering, sponsored by the NCCB, raised up the many cultures and ethnic groups within the U.S. Church and recognized in a very prophetic way the role of faith and culture. Perhaps more than any other event, this moment in the life of the Church in the U.S. provided us with a look at who we are as Church and how we can celebrate our identity. To say it was a cultural diversity program would be undermining the richness of being "in God's House." While the significance of this event in the community of faith continues to be unpacked, we are discovering the challenges and the opportunities for us as a multicultural Church to realize our unity in God's love. The depth of the challenges and opportunities will only be fully realized when we experience the fullness of *Encuentro 2000* in our parishes and in the daily life of the local community. In order to do this, it is necessary to discover and embrace the gift of diversity in our Church, that is, the presence of people of many cultures in our faith community.

For purposes of the present discussion, the place to begin is with the question, "Who is the Latino community?" We can look first to the history of the Hispanic/Latino people. It is always helpful to see how a community is defined by its history, and this is especially important in looking at the Latino people in the Church. Their sense of history is something that is essential to the Latino community's identity. Those in the Spanish-speaking world are keenly aware of the ongoing connection between the past and the present. As for future matters, Latino culture tends to put the future confidently into the hands of God: "el hombre pone, Dios dispone" (man proposes, God disposes). This attitude seems to be in contrast to the futuristic focus prevalent in U.S. society, where planning and projecting guide decision-making, with the aim of influencing the out-come of what is yet to be.

The ongoing dialogue with history is perhaps based on the creation of a new race. In the case of the Latino community, the creation of a new race came about through the violent conquest of the native peoples by the Spanish Conquistadores. This experience has greatly affected how Latinos have come to de-fine themselves within their own culture and to some extent, in society. For instance, the need for conquest has had an influ-ence on Latino culture. Unfortunately, the need for conquest has manifested itself in family relationships (i.e., domestic violence) and in other abusive ways. While I would not say the need for conquest is characteristic of Latino culture, it nonethe-less exists and is not uncommon in far too many Latino house-holds. Placed in the context of justice, we must not only examine such social issues of Latinos, but we must make ef-forts to address them. This is appropriately done within the Church community, as well as in schools and in public forums.

The more redeeming aspects of Latino history, however, are that of faith and hope. For Mexican Americans, their experi-ence of faith and hope has greatly been shaped by their devo-tion to Our Lady of Guadalupe. As Father Virgil Elizondo points out, the Guadalupe experience is where Mexican Americans find solace and strength. It is the Mother of God who shares their sufferings, comforts and liberates them, so that they see themselves as having dignity and a mission.[1]

As opposed to the experience in the U.S. in which the indi-genous people were kept separated and isolated on reserva-tions, the Latino experience was that of interaction. The Latino people are "mestizo," the blending of the conqueror and the conquered. This is the tension, the irony, the "both/and" that de-fines the Latino community. Both sides of this tension continue

---

[1] Father Virgil Elizondo has written extensively on this topic. See espe-cially *Galilean Journey: The Mexican-American Promise* (Maryknoll, N.Y.: Orbis Books, 1983) and *The Future is Mestizo: Life Where Cultures Meet* (Oak Park, Ill.: Meyer-Stone Books, 1988), in which he beautifully describes the Mexican American experience of God, particularly in the context of the Guadalupe experience.

to be present in their lived experience as a community, as well in the home and in public life.

For Latinos, to speak conceptually of "liberation" is not to speak of the goal as being the end of a struggle; rather, there is something else for which the people are liberated, i.e., the building of God's kingdom. Thus, when or if people are "liberated" does not mean they are free of the trials of human life. Rather, from the perspective of Latinos, they are restored and are now "on par" with people who have not been oppressed. The Latino people have discovered and have claimed (or reclaimed) their human dignity, so they can join in the salvific mission of the Gospel, not solely for themselves but for the entire human community. Thus, liberation is rightfully a part of how Latino people live their lives as a people of faith and hope. It is because of this that the Latino community must share its gift of grace with the entire Church in the U.S., and it is in the parish liturgy that this gift must find its expression.

In the U.S., the Latino community has refrained from using the term "liberation" in its experience. Perhaps Latinos do not want to undermine the severe conditions of their brothers and sisters in Latin America, given the freedom and prosperity enjoyed in the U.S. Yet, I would contend that Latinos' need for liberation must be considered, so they can live out the call to justice and not be regarded solely as a political force with the potential to determine election outcomes. Rather, the Latino community must be recognized as a social force, as people who can work for change in unjust systems. As a community, Latinos are also a spiritual force, enabling them to bring the Gospel to others and to live in God's presence in the eucharistic community. What I am suggesting is that the Latino community can be regarded as a present-day model of Christian practice in the Church and U.S. society. Because of the Latino people's history, they are able to show how both struggles and joys can be integrated into the whole of life. In other words, they model how to live the "both/and" tension. I call this way of being "Fiesta Catholicism."

At a fiesta, people come together to celebrate; they eat, drink, sing, and enjoy the presence of one another. In the absence of any one of these elements, it is not a fiesta. A fiesta is comprehensive, welcoming, and inclusive. The concept of Fiesta Catholics stands in contrast to another commonly used term in today's Church, that is, "cafeteria Catholics." "Cafeteria Catholics" choose particular features of the Church, go off, and take into themselves only what they have selected. The cafeteria approach to a life of faith seems rather sterile, and it lacks the fullness of life and spirit. In liturgical celebrations, "cafeteria Catholics" feel they only have to show up, with little thought being given to the experience when they leave. In contrast, Fiesta Catholics engage in the celebration, finding the experience nourishing and life-giving. Fiesta Catholics have a commitment not only to enjoy the celebration but also to contribute to it in order to make it complete. For Latinos, the sense of being Fiesta Catholics calls us to integrate our culture and spirituality with social action. As Virgil Elizondo writes, "In the fiesta, Mexican-American rises above the quest for theological meaning of life and celebrates the very contradictions that are of the essence of the mystery of human life."[2]

Oftentimes, the divisions within the Catholic Church today are labeled as differences between the "conservatives" and the "liberals." Conservatives supposedly adhere to devotions (Mary, the saints, etc.) and are concerned about the cultivation of inner spirituality and traditional Catholic identity. The stereotype also portrays conservatives as people who see charity as something virtuous. The work of justice, on the other hand, is considered secular and consequently, something in which the Church should not involve itself. In contrast, liberals supposedly need not bother with such things as the Blessed Mother, novenas, penitential fasting (unless it is for nuclear disarmament), or admiration for the pope; the sole focus of the Church is working on sociopolitical issues and action.

In my brief time of working for the Church at the national level, I think the tension of conservative versus liberal is becoming increasingly noticeable and in my opinion, destructive. In some respects, this liberal-conservative tension might be described as a demand for "either/or," which notably contrasts with the Hispanic desire for "both/and." It is clear that where

[2] *Galilean Journey,* 43.

God's goodness is sure to occur, the evil one is hard at work to divide us in our work in building the kingdom of God. The prayer of Jesus in the Gospel of John, "that they may be one," pertains not only to ecumenical affairs but to our own realization as a community of believers of healing and redemption in every aspect of Church life. This must be embraced at every level, but ultimately it begins and finds fulfillment in the parish liturgy, which is both the means and end.

With respect to the experience of Latinos, parish liturgists and/or liturgy committees can and will have a significant impact in determining how the unity of the Church is manifested in parish life. This unity cannot be expressed solely by addressing the issue of how to serve and pastoral and liturgical needs of the Latino community, for when this is perceived as the sole issue, the immediate solution tends to be having a Mass in Spanish. Rather, the critical question to be asked is how the Latino experience can contribute to the transformation of our community of faith. The answer to this question is more complex.

The Latino experience of living the "both/and" tension is a way of being and thus, an opportunity to model the integration of spirituality and social action. Some might recall Cesar Chavez's work with the farm workers in the 1970s and 1980s. His dedication to civil rights and his devotion to the Blessed Mother (Our Lady of Guadalupe) went hand in hand in the many marches and organizing efforts in which he was involved. He often participated in the celebration of the Eucharist before beginning a march and/or fast, and he would have a banner of Our Lady of Guadalupe lead the way. Perhaps skeptics and those unfamiliar with Latino heritage would charge that this was done with political motivations. I suggest, however, that it be understood as an experience of Fiesta Catholicism.

Of course, Archbishop Oscar Romero of San Salvador could also be considered as embracing the "both/and" tension. Many are aware of his courageous efforts in speaking out against the violence and bloodshed that oppressed the poor. Many might assume that he was a proponent of liberation theology, but I doubt that he would have placed himself in this category. His commitment to the teachings of the Church and his religious piety went hand in hand with his steadfast advocacy for the poor.

There are many other courageous and devout women and men of every cultural background in our faith communities who embody Fiesta Catholicism. Those who embody the "both/and" way of being and point to true liberation need to be part of liturgical planning, so that our eucharistic celebrations are the one true expression of what our Lord instituted at the Last Supper.

The Challenge

I think all of this leads to a process of considering ways that are appropriate for how we as a Church in the U.S. become a true community. Liturgists have an extremely critical role of guiding this process. They need to see this as an opportunity to grow together in our life in Christ. Becoming a true community of faith has often been regarded as a challenge, but I believe the Holy Spirit always finds ways to transform the challenges into true moments of grace. The responsibility of Church leaders is to ensure the fullness of eucharistic worship, so that it truly unites us as the body of Christ. Of course, this can only be done when the realities of life are part of the celebrations, which in turn can bring about conversion and transformation for the entire assembly.

Practical Considerations

In order to be effective with preparing liturgies in a parish with a Latino population, I suggest that parish liturgists develop a process of listening so they might become engaged in the reality of the Latino community. It would be helpful to develop ways of becoming aware of the life of the Latino community aside from information found in statistics and textbooks. Some liturgists will see the benefit of learning Spanish, so as to communicate more effectively. However, perhaps for some, the utility is in listening rather than in correct pronunciation of words. The basic elements of such a listening process are as follows:

- *Cultural Awareness.* Know who your community is and where the people come from. Learn about their history and conditions of country/countries of origin. What is their experience in the U.S.? How can the community cherish and value its heritage in communal prayer and worship?

- *Religious Awareness.* What are some of the devotions of the community and how can they be expressed in a manner that connects with their cultural roots, as well as with their present day reality? It is worth looking into the role of popular religiosity for the non-Hispanic members of a multicultural parish.

- *Sociopolitical/Economic Awareness.* What are some of the issues being faced by the community (e.g., housing, immigration, health, etc.) that can be incorporated into the life of prayer and the life of action (e.g., community organizing, legislative advocacy, etc.)?

- *Awareness of Opportunities.* What are opportunities for collaboration, learning, and unity by various cultures in community? How does this get expressed in the prayer life of the Church? In addition, what are the leadership needs and models that present themselves?

Examples

Latino cultures offer a multitude of occasions for celebration and commemoration. Traditions vary in each culture, but the majority of these traditions have religious roots. Although the associations of certain customs might seem to have lost their meaning outside of the country of origin, efforts can be made to enhance the celebration and commemoration in the new context of life in the United States. Furthermore, the custom or event need not be limited to the Latino community. Liturgy provides for universal expression, so all people may find meaning in its message. The following are two familiar traditions of Mexican origin that speak to timeless themes in U.S. society:

- *Our Lady of Guadalupe.* This celebration of the apparition of the Mother of God holds a special place for the entire community. What she represents is the true dignity of every person and true unity in her son, Jesus. Parishes across the U.S. have begun to have special liturgical celebrations of this special day. These celebrations can raise the awareness of the prophetic witness within our own community and our fidelity to building the Church in our own locale.

- *Quinceañeras.* As a celebration of a girl's fifteenth birthday, the origin of this tradition has been variously ascribed: indigenous puberty rites, *criollo* coming-out parties, etc. However, in preparing for the celebration as well as in the actual liturgy, this is a time to address the dignity of women. The focus is not solely on the quinceañera (fifteen-year-old girl) but includes an opportunity for the entire community to reflect on its role in upholding the values that support the esteem of women in all aspects of society. It is also an opportunity for all (men and women) to commit to a life of purity and wholeness and of service to others.

Undoubtedly, part of the challenge at times may be in the willingness of the Latino community to share these customs and to allow for the universal message(s) to be amplified. For liturgists and others, it may be the way to initiate dialogue, which will hopefully be fruitful in many respects. It might also be the beginning of mutual participation in the work of unity. In this way, we can learn from one another, as we reflect on how the gifts of the Latino community contribute to the unity of all the members of the Church in the Most Holy Trinity.

C. Vanessa White

Liturgy as a Liberating Force

I'm gonna move when the Spirit say move
I'm gonna move when the Spirit say move
When the Spirit say move
I'm gonna move Oh Lord
I'm gonna move when the Spirit say move

African American Spiritual

Black people are a Spirit-filled people. This religious nature of black people has been, as Gayraud Wilmore states, "an essential thread in the fabric of Black culture," which transcends regional differences and socioeconomic backgrounds.[1] It is our sense of this Spirit that has helped us as African Americans to survive centuries of oppression, alienation, floggings, lynchings, discrimination, murder, and human devaluation. It is that Spirit of God that has helped us to survive as a people. In the midst of all our struggles, and they are many, we have moved onward and upward. Evidence of the strength of that binding thread of Spirit is the continued authentic expression of personal and communal prayer, specifically as seen in our liturgical celebrations.

African American spirituality is at the root of our liturgy. In the NCCB document *Plenty Good Room: The Spirit and Truth of*

---

[1] Gayraud S. Wilmore, *Black Religion and Black Radicalism*, 2nd ed. (Maryknoll, N.Y.: Orbis Books, 1983) 220.

African American Catholic Worship, it is written that spirituality must be the starting point of a distinctively African American Catholic liturgy.[2] To understand us as a people and to understand our liturgy, one must understand our spirituality. Our spirituality is not an excuse but a reason for our survival. Our spirituality has African roots. The ways of searching for God and experiencing God's presence in our lives is not done within a vacuum but a cultural context. Fr. Cyprian Davis says that the context of a black spirituality is the African experience lived out in America.[3]

Further, Caryle Stewart Fielding writes in *Soul Survivors* that "African American spirituality has been instrumental in giving black people the spiritual and cultural elements to liberate themselves from those internal tyrannies that sequester the soul and destroy the mind."[4] If liturgy celebrates the landscapes of human experience—happiness, sadness, grief, and renewal—then the liturgy must touch upon our human experience, which is expressed in the context of our spirituality. Writing about black spirituality, Sr. Jamie T. Phelps observes:

> Black spirituality is a vital and distinctive spirituality forged in the crucible of the lives of various African peoples. . . . This common spirit found in peoples of African descent is an attitude that sees all of life in the context of the encounter with the Divine, and the all embracing vision of the Divine-human encounter—which is really the essential clue to understanding the nature of black spirituality—is rooted in a distinctive and ancient world view.[5]

If in worship, African Americans are allowed to celebrate and worship God in a manner that speaks to us, then that worship

[2] NCCB, *Plenty Good Room: The Spirit and Truth of African American Catholic Worship* (Washington, D.C.: USCC, 1990) 48.

[3] Cyprian Davis, "Some Reflections on African American Catholic Spirituality," *U.S. Catholic Historian* (Spring 2001) 8.

[4] Carlyle Fielding Stewart III, *Soul Survivors* (Louisville, Ky.: Westminster John Knox Press, 1997) 23.

[5] Jamie Phelps, "Black Spirituality" in *Spiritual Traditions for the Contemporary Church,* eds. Robin Maas and Gabriel O'Donnell (Nashville: Abingdon Press, 1990) 332.

is liberating, calling us to transformation. But what are the components of a black spirituality? How is it defined and expressed? What is the impact of black spirituality on liturgy celebrated in the black community?

Components of Black Spirituality

GOD CENTERED

God is the lens through which people of African descent experience all things. Our God-view orchestrates, governs, empowers, transforms, and infuses us with a soul that is the basis and the power of our life. In Western culture, the theological question has been "Is there a God?" The question for black people was never "Is there a God?" but rather, "How is God present in the midst of my suffering, my joy?" When we get up in the morning we say "thank you Jesus." Our grandmothers and grandfathers, our aunts and uncles—all of our ancestors—testified to the power of God in their lives. Our sense of God is the basis and power of life. God is both immanent and transcendent; God dwells within us and is beyond us. Such phrases as "God don't ever change" and "There will always be a God" infuse our language and speak of our concept of God. As a director of a graduate theological program for African American Catholics studying for lay ecclesial ministry, I am struck by how often my students speak of being called by God and use God language in their everyday communications. They speak of that sense of God as always present. For black people, our sense of God is as natural as breathing.

BIBLICALLY ROOTED

Black spirituality is based on the sacred Scriptures. As stated by the black bishops of the U.S. in their pastoral letter on evangelization in the black community, *What We Have Seen and Heard,* "The Bible story is our story; the Bible promise is our hope."[6]

---

[6] Black Bishops of the United States, *What We Have Seen and Heard: Pastoral Letter on Evangelization* (Cincinnati: St. Anthony Messenger Press, 1984) 5.

I come from an ecumenical family. Within my extended family I am blessed to have members from a variety of faith traditions, including Methodist, Catholic, Apostolic, AME Zion, and Lutheran. While our faith traditions are different, the one characteristic we have in common aside from our belief in Jesus Christ, is a love and knowledge of Scripture. When I was a child, my family began meals with prayer, which included a Bible verse. In our family gatherings, we testify to the power of God's Word in our lives. The Bible was not foreign to us. As a black people, the Bible story was our story. The spirituals are biblically rooted. Our ancestors who were forcibly brought to the U.S. connected with the Exodus story. Even when the slave masters tried to convince our ancestors that God condoned their enslavement because the "Bible says so," they knew that the God of Jesus Christ did not call them to be slaves and that the master had the wrong interpretation of the Holy Scripture. Jesus said that the truth would set us free. The Bible promise is our promise. It is an instrument of our spiritual empowerment.

JOYFUL, HOLISTIC AND CONTEMPLATIVE

Joy is a hallmark of black spirituality.[7] We celebrate in the midst of suffering. Our joy does not negate the suffering but is focused on the belief in the hope of Jesus Christ. Our joy is expressed in our movement, our dance, our song, in color and sensation, in thanksgiving and exultation.

Black spirituality is holistic. Feelings are not separate from intellect; the heart is not separate from the soul. Black people use their bodies to express their love of God. There is not a separation of the sacred and the secular. Divisions between intellect and emotion, spirit and body, action and contemplation, individual and community, or sacred and secular are foreign to us.[8]

Black people are a contemplative people. We experience God at all times and in many ways. Prayer is both spontaneous and pervasive in our community, and every place is a place of

[7] Ibid., 9.
[8] Ibid., 8.

prayer. This sense of God's presence taught us that no one can run from God, nor can anyone hide from God.

COMMUNITY/PERSON FOCUSED

In West African tradition, the "I" is defined in the "we." Our individual identity is to be found in the context of the community. This communal aspect of our spirituality is quite evident in our churches and at our liturgies. One cannot enter an authentically black church and not feel welcome. Several years ago, I was responsible for organizing Alternative Spring Break Experiences with college students. These experiences were to introduce students to different cultures and give them the opportunity to reflect on the social structures within the U.S. This experience included taking the youth (who were primarily white) to an African American Catholic church for Sunday Mass. The students were repeatedly struck by the hospitality and sense of community they experienced, which for many was quite unlike what they had experienced in their home parishes. Many commented that if the experience were reversed, they would question whether the people of St. Benedict the African West would be welcome in their home parish. Hospitality and community are gifts of black folk. All are welcome in the Father's house.

At the same, it must be recognized that the black community is multifaceted and not monolithic. There are diverse preferences within our corporate spirituality. As Sr. Thea Bowman states, "ministers who wish to know how to interpret, relate and impact the spirituality of Black people, must endeavor to learn the reality of a particular group of Black people their ministry effects."[9]

JUSTICE-LIBERATION ORIENTED

The community-person focus of black spirituality impacts how we treat one another. The quality of a person's life is

---

[9] Thea Bowman, "Spirituality: The Soul of the People," *Tell It Like It Is* (Oakland, Calif.: National Black Sisters Conference) 85.

important. Jesus' message is one of establishing right relationships—in other words, establishing the reign of God. As Christians, we are called to prophetic action on behalf of justice. We
cannot remain quiet when we experience injustice. This is the
testament of St. Sabina's Catholic Church, a black Catholic
parish on the south side of Chicago. The community of St.
Sabina recently was challenged to live their spirituality when
they were denied membership in the Southside Catholic Conference (a predominately white amateur athletic association).
This community could not remain silent or inactive when they
experienced this injustice. The parish is working with other
churches in the Chicago area in hope of reconciliation and
healing.[10]

Sr. Jamie Phelps says that the absolute criterion of the au-
thenticity of black spirituality is the following: "Do the actions
of the community lead to right relationships? Does the person
act right and call others to be right? Does the person and the
community struggle for the liberation of oppressed persons,
races and nations?"[11] A person and a community imbued with
the life force, the Spirit of God, that is at the center of black
spirituality is willing to struggle for liberation from sin and its
effects.

African American liturgies, therefore, must express the spirituality of black people. They should not only facilitate the dis-
covery of new insights and meanings, but also challenge us to
live life anew as disciples. All should recognize themselves
when Christ is present. Liturgy that does not have meaning for
the community is dead. It will not be transformative, nor will it
be liberating. If liturgy does not address the Spirit of God, the

---

[10] St. Sabina Catholic Church is a black Catholic parish on the south side
of Chicago, pastored by white diocesan priest, Rev. Michael Pfleger, and
known for its vibrant liturgies, ecumenical stance, strong lay leadership
development, and social action. With Fr. George Clements (black Catholic
diocesan priest, founder of One Church, One Child) in the 1980s and
1990s, St. Sabina's was active in the dismantling of billboards that focused
on alcohol and cigarette advertising in the black community.

[11] From class lectures given by Jamie Phelps, O.P., at the Institute of
Black Catholic Studies, Xavier University, New Orleans.

Catholic faith, and the lived reality of black people (our spirituality), then liturgy will not have the power to transform and liberate. As Melva Wilson Costa writes in *African American Christian Worship*, "No participation in ritual action, whether culturally understood or borrowed from other cultures, can be renewing if the intent of the Christ event is not rooted in a true desire of the worshipper to be transformed."[12]

During liturgy, we again experience the paschal mystery, which calls us to live life anew, that is, transformed, and to once again experience God's self-giving and liberating act through our Lord Jesus Christ. Is the liturgy from the beginning to the end of the liturgical celebration (the proclamation of the Word, the homily, the intercessory prayers, the sign of peace, the eucharistic prayer, the hymns, the opening and closing prayers, and dismissal) transforming and liberating? Does our public worship speak to the lived experience of black people and as a result, of the liberating and transformative experience of liturgy? Do we go forth as a community, in the words of Bishop Terry Steib, "revived, renewed and ready" to proclaim the liberating Good News of Jesus Christ?[13]

[12] Melva Wilson Costen. *African American Christian Worship* (Nashville: Abingdon Press, 1993) 128.

[13] At the closing liturgy for the Black Catholic Congress in 1992, Bishop Terry Steib (ordinary of Memphis, Tennessee) used the terminology "revived, renewed and ready" to speak of the experience of attending the Congress.

| *Mary Alice Piil*, C.S.J. |

Liturgy as the Church's Spirituality: A School of Discipleship

The Spiritual Quest

The question of spirituality is very much on the minds of Americans today. After the tragic events of September 11, 2001 —the terrorist attacks in New York City and Washington, D.C.— many have gathered to remember loved ones and to gain strength from one another in the face of an uncertain future. The questions as to why have no answers. All are struggling to find new meaning in life as they encourage and comfort one another. The environment is ripe for evangelization. Yet, we must realize that the call to conversion and a change of heart will be challenged by the many factors that have influenced and continue to influence the typical Christian today.

Prior to September 11 there were signs all around us of a renewed search for the spiritual. Aroma therapy, meditation music, health spas abound provided opportunities for the seeker to escape the pressures of modern society and attempt to answer some of the questions of meaning of life. One needed to watch but a few hours of television for advice: Be true to yourself; get away from it all; you owe it to yourself; you need time for yourself. As many sought new expressions for their spiritual search, the influence of the culture was too often quite evident. The radical individualism of the typical American

117

found expression in a variety of forms, with a very private, personal prayer being but one of them. It is interesting to see just how one event can change a people's focus. On September 11, a whole city became centered on the other rather than on the self. People asked: How can I help? What can I do to alleviate the suffering of the other? Where can I go for answers to such unspeakable terror? Many people turned to their local church for the answers, making it clear that the old approaches were not satisfactory.

The crisis of spirituality, evident for several decades now, continues. Prior to September 11, this search was too often evident in lifestyle changes that further complicate the search for the meaning of life. For instance, priority was often given to the achievement of individual success and independence. Typically, the successful individual has been encouraged to deny death no matter what its face. Some found cults which lure the seeker to be an escape. Others retreated to past practices that speak of simpler times when all was well with the world.

However, we in the U.S. do not live in the world of the past but rather twenty-first century America! In the face of terror and death, many people had nowhere to turn. Faced with the reality of a tragic death, many tried to pray, only to discover that they did not know how. Prayer, or a prayer tradition, is not a value to the typical middle-class lifestyle of many Americans. The traditional structures of family life that supported the development of a healthy individual are in crisis. The significant others necessary to assist in the development of a strong religious identity are lacking. In the Roman Catholic community today, young adults often ask questions that indicate a lack of catholic identity. In reality, what they desire is what might be termed a true "catholic spirituality."

We are certainly not lacking in forms of spirituality in the Church today. Many of the very successful renewal programs that have helped many to discover their baptismal identity suggest a particular spirituality. The typical parish bulletin suggests that various prayer groups following one or another prayer form are available to serve the needs of our diverse congregations. Unfortunately, while the variety of experiences has often made a positive contribution to renewal of individuals, they tend to build upon the American spirit of individualism by focusing on the needs of the "I." Any sense of concern for the poor and needy outside one's own small world is not evident. Thus, these forms of spirituality, though perhaps necessary as part of a larger picture, do not lead to authentic Christian spirituality.

Christian Spirituality and Liturgical Life

The question is therefore asked: "What is Christian spirituality?" Elizabeth Dreyer offers this definition: "Christian spirituality is the daily, communal, lived expression of one's ultimate beliefs characterized by openness to the self-transcending love of God, self, neighbor and world through Jesus Christ and in the power of the Spirit. 'Spirituality' is a term that describes realities related to the Spirit of God."[1] Clearly, such a definition offers a holistic approach in which the self and the world are not divided into compartments, as was so often true in forms of spirituality offered in the past. Human development is key to this view of spirituality; the whole person—body, mind, and spirit—is engaged.

It is in keeping with the long tradition of the Church that such spirituality, if it is to take root and flourish, must flow from an active liturgical life. Shawn Madigan describes "liturgical spirituality" as:

> the participation of a faith community in God's creative and transformative love for the world. Christian liturgical spirituality is the community's participation in the liberating embrace of the world in, with, and through Jesus Christ. "God has given us the wisdom to understand fully the mystery, the plan that was decreed in Christ, to be carried out in the fullness of time" (Eph 1:9-10).

> Though the paschal mystery of Jesus Christ is at the heart of all Christian spirituality, liturgical spirituality is formed and

[1] Elizabeth Dreyer, "Christian Spirituality," in *Encyclopedia of Catholicism,* ed. Richard McBrien (New York: HaperCollins Publishers, 1995) 1216.

informed through the ritual celebrations of the paschal mystery. Though all Christians celebrate the cultic liturgy of the church, Christians who live a liturgical spirituality experience the liturgical life of the church as their source of spiritual direction. For these Christians, the cultic liturgy of the church clearly is "the summit toward which the activity of the church is directed" and "the fountain from which all her power flows" (SC 10).[2]

Significant to the above definition is the focus on the liturgy celebrated as the source of spiritual direction, i.e., the direction for life of the individual Christian. This was in fact the goal of the Fathers of the Second Vatican Council, whose vision of liturgical reform included this particular need. It is helpful to reread with an eye toward present concerns the first article of the Constitution on the Sacred Liturgy:

This Sacred Council has several aims in view: it desires to impart an ever increasing vigor to the Christian life of the faithful; to adapt more suitably to the needs of our times those institutions that are subject to change; to foster whatever can promote union among all who believe in Christ; to strengthen whatever can help to call the whole of humanity into the household of the Church. The Council therefore sees particularly cogent reasons for undertaking the reform and promotion of the liturgy. For the liturgy . . . is the outstanding means whereby the faithful may express in their lives and manifest to others the mystery of Christ and the real nature of the true Church.[3]

It is clear that the goal of the council was to connect the Christian life with participation in the liturgy. The liturgy is to express a reality that is being lived, i.e., the Christian life. Yet, it is also to be the font from which one would receive the strength necessary to go forth and live the paschal mystery in the modern world.

Rather than the liturgy itself being the starting point for the conversation about spirituality, we begin with the mystery of

---

[2] S. Shawn Madigan, "Liturgical Spirituality," in *The New Dictionary of Sacramental Worship,* ed. Peter E. Fink (Collegeville: The Liturgical Press, 1990) 1224–25.

[3] SC 1.

Christ and the real nature of the true Church. But we ask: Who is the Church? The answer: The Body of Christ here in this world, carrying out Christ's mission. While Christ and his Church are the starting point, we must go to the actual liturgical celebration in order to experience this reality in its fullness. The Church experiences its identity as it gathers to celebrate the Eucharist. This relationship between the life of the Christian and the celebration of that life in the liturgy has been the focus of pastoral liturgists for decades. Consider again the words of the council:

> For the liturgy, through which "the work of our redemption is accomplished," most of all in the divine sacrifice of the Eucharist, is the outstanding means whereby the faithful may express in their lives and manifest to others the mystery of Christ and the real nature of the true Church. It is of the essence of the Church that she be both human and divine, visible and yet invisibly equipped, eager to act and yet intent on contemplation, present in this world and yet not at home in it; and she is all these things in such ways that in her the human is directed and subordinated to the divine, the visible likewise to the invisible, action to contemplation, and this present world to that city yet to come, which we seek (cf. Heb 13:14). While the liturgy daily builds up those who are within into a holy temple of the Lord, into a dwelling place for God in the Spirit (cf. Eph 2:21-22), to the mature measure of the fullness of Christ (cf. Eph 4:13), at the same time it marvelously strengthens their power to preach Christ, and thus shows forth the Church to those who are outside as a sign lifted up among the nations (cf. Is 11:12) under which the scattered children of God may be gathered together (cf. Jn 11:52), until there is one sheepfold and one shepherd (cf. Jn 10:16).[4]

Following then from the reforms of the council, two elements are essential to a renewed Christian spirituality: that the individual Christian enter into the paschal mystery, which is manifest particularly in the eucharistic liturgy, and that the individual do so within the context of the Church, i.e., "the Church here and now assembled."

---

[4] SC 2 (footnotes omitted).

In the celebration of the liturgy, the paschal mystery, the dying and rising of Christ, is made present. Transcending time and space, the risen Lord is actually present to the worshipping community, making it possible for the Christian to respond to the ultimate gift of redemption. As the Church remembers *(anamnesis)* the passion, death, and resurrection of Christ, we are challenged to enter into the saving mystery. The faithful are called upon to die with Christ and share in the resurrection to new life. Christ provides the model of a life of self-offering. All Christians are called to model their lives on his through active engagement in the liturgical act. This participation is real and actual, that is, the individual through making an offering of self, of dying to a life of self-centeredness and putting on the mind of Christ, is given the gift of living life anew in Christ's embrace.

A Liturgical Spirituality and the Call to Discipleship

Volumes have been written concerning the fundamental reality that the Vatican II Church has as its starting point the Church made manifest in the local community. The baptized, those who have committed themselves to a life of discipleship in Christ, live life in communion in the power of the Spirit. Essential to the Catholic/Christian identity is the sense of being one Body of Christ. There is no Christian without first coming into contact with the Church. It is through participation in the very life of the Christian community that one comes to discover what it means to be a Christian. But this concept of Christian community is not without its challenges. Over the centuries complacency has crept in, or even more challenging, a romantic concept of what community might be for the individual. Christian identity entails a personal commitment. However, "this identity does not bypass the church as institution. Christian identity is not self-administered. . . ."[5] Dietrich Bonhoeffer in *Life Together* offers this perspective:

---

[5] Louis-Marie Chauvet, *Symbol and Sacrament,* Madeleine M. Beaumont and Patrick Madigan, trans. (Collegeville: The Liturgical Press, 1999) 31.

> In Christian brotherhood everything depends upon its being
> clear right from the beginning, *first, that Christian brotherhood is
> not an ideal, but a divine reality. Second, that Christian brotherhood is
> a spiritual and not a psychic reality. . . .* Every human dream
> wish that is injected into the Christian community is a hin-
> drance to genuine community and must be banished if genuine
> community is to survive. He who loves his dream of a commu-
> nity more than the Christian community itself becomes a de-
> stroyer of the latter, even though his personal intentions may be
> ever so honest and earnest and sacrificial.[6]

Significant then to an understanding of liturgical spirituality
is an understanding of the Church as mystery. Rather than con-
ceiving of the Church solely as a social institution, although it
is clear that its horizontal dimension must be recognized, the
Church as sacrament must be highlighted. In his groundbreak-
ing study, *Symbol and Sacrament*, Louis-Marie Chauvet states it
succinctly:

> Living in God, the Lord Jesus has left his place on earth as the
> story of the Ascension shows. From now on, this place is occu-
> pied by the church. Of course the church occupies this place
> symbolically, that is, by maintaining the radical difference, for
> the church is not Christ, but his symbolic witness, which means
> that its original and constant raison d'être is to direct everything
> back to him. It is in the church that faith finds its structure be-
> cause the church is in charge of keeping alive, in the midst of
> the world and for its good, the memory through the Scriptures,
> read and interpreted as speaking about him or being his own
> living word; memory through the sacraments, (here the break-
> ing of the bread) recognized as being his own salvific gestures;
> memory through the ethical testimony of mutual sharing, lived
> as an expression of his own service of humankind.[7]

Chauvet offers the challenge that had been so much a part of the
early liturgical reformers, that is, to connect liturgy and social

---

[6] Dietrich Bonhoeffer, *Life Together* (London: S.C.M., 1954) 26–27, as
quoted in Mark Searle, "On the Art of Lifting Up the Heart: Liturgical
Prayer Today," *Studies in Formative Spirituality* 3:3 (1982) 402 (emphasis
original).

[7] Chauvet, 28.

justice. Stated differently, the challenge is to see word, sacrament, and ethics as sacramental, and to help the individual Christian realize that the intimate relationship between the life of discipleship and the liturgy cannot be broken. As the Constitution on the Sacred Liturgy states:

> Nevertheless, the liturgy is the summit toward which the activity of the Church is directed; at the same time it is the font from which all her power flows. For the aim and object of apostolic works is that all who are made sons of God by faith and Baptism should come together to praise God in the midst of his Church, to take part in the sacrifice and to eat the Lord's Supper. The liturgy in its turn moves the faithful, filled with "the paschal sacraments," to be "one in holiness"; it prays that "they may hold fast in their lives to what they have grasped by their faith"; the renewal in the Eucharist of the covenant between the Lord and man draws the faithful into the compelling love of Christ and sets them on fire. From the liturgy, therefore, and especially from the Eucharist, as from a font, grace is poured forth upon us, and the sanctification of men in Christ and the glorification of God, to which all other activities of the Church are directed as toward their end, is achieved in the most efficacious possible way.[8]

The challenge to bring all members of the Church to an understanding of this dynamic between the Church at prayer and the Church carrying out the mission of Christ in the world has been at the heart of the twentieth-century reforms. To illustrate, the constant call of modern popes has been one of making connections between the life of prayer and the life of discipleship. For example, Pius XII in *Mediator Dei* recognized the need to interiorize the externals. Romano Guardini, one of the great spiritual writers of the twentieth century asked how we can make the external act an epiphany and how the very doing of the liturgy can be for the participant an in-breaking of the holy.[9]

[8] SC 10 (footnotes omitted).
[9] Romano Guardini, "A Letter from Romano Guardini," *Assembly* (April 1986) 323.

A modern theology of prayer must be rooted in a sacramental theology that flows from the Church's understanding of self as sacrament. No longer is prayer divorced from the sacramental life of the Church. The approach to prayer of the traditional "spiritualities" needs to be rethought as a result of the recovery of an understanding of the paschal mystery and our participation in that mystery. At every level, connections must be made that will encourage the individual member of the assembly to see that one's relationship with Christ is intimately bound to one's participation in the life of the Church. This message is not new; it has been offered for decades. But has the message fallen on deaf ears or were we not ready to grasp the full scope of the need to radically rethink the spirituality of the person in the assembly? Much has happened in these forty years since the initial stages of the reform of liturgical books. It is now clear that the reform of the liturgical rites is a mere beginning. If the rituals found in the books are to have lasting effects in the lives of the Christian community, more needs to be accomplished. The interiorization called for by Pius XII is needed more than ever. Guardini's challenge of nearly forty years ago needs to be heeded.

Here, we can ask: How can we make the proclamation of the Word a true encounter with the risen Lord? How can we prepare the Liturgy of the Eucharist so that all the baptized are engaged in a profound experience of Christ present? How can the assembly be challenged to move from the celebration of word and sacrament to active participation in the Church's mission of justice in the world today?

Christ is present in the proclamation of the Word within the context of the gathered assembly, which challenges this generation of Christians to be transformed anew in the Spirit. God's presence is freely and powerfully given to all who encounter Christ's presence in Word. The Word that is addressed to the baptized demands a response. This response entails going forth and proclaiming this saving Word to others. As the believer encounters Christ, she or he is moved to follow his example. Just as Christ embraced the cross in order that we might have life, so too does the faithful Christian respond to the challenge to look at life anew, as Christ would see it. Each individual is challenged to evaluate the personal response to Gospel values. Each becomes aware of those areas of life which are in need of transformation, if one is to continue to be Christ's presence in the world today. In dying to all that is not of God, the believer rises to new life in the Spirit. The words of Chauvet, in speaking of the Emmaus account, are again instructive:

> If it is indeed the foundational discourse of the church (its kerygma) we perceive here behind the discourse of the risen Jesus on the Scriptures, the issue which dominates the whole of our story becomes clear: you cannot arrive at the recognition of the risen Jesus unless you renounce seeing/touching/finding him by undeniable proofs. Faith begins precisely with such a renunciation of the immediacy of the see/know and with the assent to the mediation of the church. For it is he the Lord, who speaks through the church each time it reads and interprets the Scriptures as referring to him or, conversely, each time it rereads Jesus' destiny of death and resurrection as "in accordance with the Scriptures." In other words, each time the assembly in church proclaims and hears the Scriptures as being his very word ("He is present in his word since it is himself who speaks when Holy Scriptures are read in church," Vatican II will declare, as the apostolic tradition had said); it is his spokesperson, his representative, therefore his sacrament.[10]

The first challenge then to those who minister to the Word in the assembly would be to understand and therefore experience the Word proclaimed as sacrament. Those called upon to proclaim the Word in the assembly—whether they be lay ministers reading the first and second readings, cantors leading the responsorial psalm, or the deacon or priest proclaiming the gospel and giving the homily—engage everyone in the assembly so that they experience the risen Lord as truly in their midst. In this dynamic encounter, each member of the assembly is able to enter into dialogue with Christ. In communion with one another, each person is able to hear anew the Gospel imperative: Go forth and bring the Gospel to all people.

The reformed Order of the Mass is structured to allow for the symbolic engagement of all members of the assembly in the

---

[10] Chauvet, 25.

proclamation. The reader (always a layperson) is called from among the assembly to witness to the fact that all are engaged in this ministry in life. The act of reading in the liturgy is a manifestation of the ongoing reality of the layperson's living out the life of discipleship daily. It is a sign to all that each member of the assembly is to follow the witness professed by the reader in the act of proclaiming the Word. A homily is an essential element in the Liturgy of the Word. The newly revised GIRM (2000) further highlights the importance of the homily by expanding the former edition (GIRM 1975) of article 42. In article 66 of GIRM 2000 we read: "There must be a homily on Sundays and holydays of obligation and it may not be omitted except for a grave reason in any Mass celebrated with a congregation."

While it is crucial that the ministers engage the assembly in the name of Christ present in the Word, it is imperative that they understand the end for which the community is engaged in this proclamation. In 1973, the U.S. Bishops offered the following challenge to ministers responsible for the formation of the assembly:

> Catechetical instruction should foster an ever-increasing awareness of the Triune God. It should enable students to grasp, through faith, the great truth that beginning at Baptism, they are called to a lifelong developing intimacy with the three divine Persons.
>
> We worship God especially in the sacred liturgy, offering ourselves to him, through our Lord Jesus Christ. We commit ourselves to carrying out his will in our every activity, and to use and increase the talents he has given to us. And from his goodness we receive the graces needed to profess the truth in love and to bring forth the fruits of love, justice and peace, all to his glory.[11]

The entire assembly needs to be formed so that each member might be engaged in the proclamation of Scripture with an end

[11] NCCB, *Basic Teachings for Catholic Religious Education* (Washington, D.C.: USCC, 1973) 128.

toward meditating on the truth presented in light of the life of discipleship. Each encounter with the Word should surface the question: Am I living as Christ in the world? Am I ready to make personal the call of Pope Paul VI, that is, "evangelization cannot be complete unless account is taken of the links between the gospel and the concrete personal and social life of men and women. . . . The Church considers it highly important to establish structures which are more human, more just, more respectful of the rights of the person, less oppressive and coercive"?[12]

Not only is the individual to meditate on the personal life of discipleship, but each member of the assembly is to dwell on the fact that it is the Church present in this local community that is being called to transform the society in which it exists. The Gospel imperative to make all things new in Christ is to be realized through the very activity of this local community in the world.

To live such a radical life of discipleship demands a strong identification with Christ and the Church. To live this commitment demands ongoing transformation of the Christian spirit. The entire assembly, having been challenged by the Word, receives the courage to go forth by placing themselves on the eucharistic table along with the bread and wine. As these simple elements are transformed into the Body and Blood of Christ, the Church prays that each of the baptized might become one with Christ in the Spirit. As Christ came to heal, redeem, and sanctify, so too the Christian filled with the Spirit goes forth to be another Christ, bringing the saving Word to a people suffering from the evils present in today's world.

[12] Pope Paul VI, *Evangelization in the Modern World* (1975) 29 and 36.

James M. Schellman

Initiation:
Forming Disciples for
Christ's Mission in the World

The *Rite of Christian Initiation of Adults* ("Rite") as implemented in many of our parishes and dioceses in the United
States and Canada is generally considered to be a success. Each
year large numbers of people can be found immersed in the
liturgical-catechetical process that the Rite embraces, from pre-
catechumenate to mystagogy and everything between. Annually, thousands are brought through the waters of baptism and
chrismation to the eucharistic table at the Easter Vigil.

What Does Success Mean?

In fact, the outward signs of success with the renewed process of adult initiation centered on the catechumenate are so great
that it is easy to overlook some of the basic questions we must
ask ourselves continually about pastoral experience with the
Rite. Is the Rite being implemented, for example, in such a way
that it respects the real spiritual journeys of the inquirers and
catechumens? Are they and the Spirit working within them
given the time and care that each individual journey of conversion requires? In other words, is the work of making Christians
a permanent, year-round process within our communities of
faith? The evidence suggests otherwise. The majority of our

parishes still do a partial year or school calendar process. It may seem a small point, but the stakes are high. The received wisdom of the Rite is frustrated by such an inflexible process. This is perhaps beginning to become apparent in the growing evidence that (1) inflexible scheduling is a primary deterrent to those who choose not to continue in the process, and (2) the rate of retention of those who have completed the process seems to decrease in parishes with a partial year approach.

Transformation: Initiation's Goal

This is just one of the fundamental and critical questions we need to be asking of our present practice. Many more could be added. I would like to suggest that many of these would be addressed if we were to step back at this juncture in the implementation of the Rite and ask ourselves the most fundamental question of all, that is, "What is the true goal of initiation?" If we get this right, I believe that all the rest will follow.

For some, the goal may be baptism. For others, Eucharist. For still others, becoming members of the Catholic faith community. Of course, there is some overlap of meaning even in these answers. But these can only be considered partial responses to the question. If we look to the General Introduction to *Christian Initiation*, we find that together baptism and confirmation bring us "to the dignity of adopted children, a new creation through water and the Spirit . . . to bear witness to him before all the world and work to bring the Body of Christ to its fullness soon as possible" (*Christian Initiation*, General Introduction, 2). Seen from this perspective, the goal of initiation is evangelization leading to transformation. And this transformation is about persons, communities, and structures, the world itself. All of us who have come through the waters and the anointing in the Spirit become "a new creation" by being transformed into members of the Body, the mystical and dynamic Body of the Lord. And this Body exists at the heart of the world and for its transformation. What else does it mean to talk of working "to bring the Body of Christ to its fullness as soon as possible"?

There is an urgency in this perspective, and it is God's. The creator, preserver, and redeemer of all that is will not be content until all that this incomparable love has created is as it was originally intended to be, transparent to and icon of God's very self. And since God's original intent was frustrated through the mystery of human sin, the means of this great evangelization is humanity itself. Made in God's image and restored to its fullness in Christ's dying and rising, we are forged into a people, Christ's own Body, present in the world and, by virtue of the One who lives within us, effecting its transformation.

We and the world we inhabit are intimately connected. We are in it but not of it in the sense that we are agents in Christ of the new creation, that which is being formed out of the old, fallen stuff we helped bring about. God does not create anything and then lose interest in it. Made out of love, we and the creation we inhabit are made for eternity, have always been intended for God. Together we are the objects of God's irrevocable regard. Isn't this the import of those magnificent words of Paul in the Letter to the Romans: "All creation is longing and groaning . . . eagerly awaiting the revelation of the children of God" (Rom 8:19-20). Creation awaits nothing less than Christ's sacramental people, his Body, being brought to their fullness *as soon as possible!* The world and its inhabitants long for this, for Christ, whether they know it or not.

Much is at stake in getting this right. The destiny of the world and humanity are the same. The first is being transformed, longingly and groaningly, into something yet unimaginable but every bit as breathtaking and beautiful as the resurrected humanity being forged in Christ. Irenaeus, our ancient and blessed forebear, had it so right: "the world itself, restored to its original state, facing no further obstacles, should be at the service of the just, sharing their glorification in the risen Jesus Christ" (*Haer*. 5.32.1).

Apprenticeship: Initiation's Means

If we do not get this right, the recovery of the initiation process underway in our parishes and dioceses will remain incomplete. The goal is not the water, anointing, nor the table. The goal is that through the waters, anointed by the Spirit, and fed at the Lord's table, we become the Lord's Body compelled to be about the Lord's business in the world. Evangelization brings one to sacramental transformation for the world and its very life. Jim Dunning, founder of The North American Forum on the Catechumenate with Christiane Brusselmans, had his own unique way of putting it: "It is not so much that the Church has a mission, but that the mission has a Church!"

Initiation holds out the promise to us of recovering this vision of Church as one of a community of disciples on mission in the world. If we keep this vision before us and let it critique our pastoral practice, the results could be remarkable. We will experience that those we are bringing into relationship with Christ will help put right the way we ourselves conceive and put that relationship into practice. We will see that the hunger, longing, and sheer need of much of our surrounding society and world make the hesitation and much of the bickering within our communities of faith not only unworthy, but verging on the scandalous. Can a household continue to wait or constantly argue when its neighboring household is under siege? By the same token, by keeping our eyes more clearly on the mission we may see how better to relate to one another, how to put our own house in proper, mission-driven order—to come to be in right relationship with one another and the world.

The catechumenate as apprenticeship in a way of life holds out great hope in this regard. On the one hand this way of formation suggests taking whatever time it takes. Look at the time we lavish on bringing the human person to maturity in the cultures of North America! Why should we treat our catechumens to less than the minimum one full year catechumenate that the Rite expects?

With the stakes for our mission as Church being as large as they are, nothing less than a true apprenticeship will do. In terms of a distinctly Christian way of perceiving and being in the world, apprenticeship suggests not only enough time, but also sufficient comprehensiveness. The catechumen-apprentice learns to be part of a Body sustaining itself and doing its work. So it is that "[The] initiation of catechumens is a gradual process that takes place *within* the community of the faithful"

(RCIA, General Introduction, 4). It is the work of the whole Body. Where that Body learns, prays, gives comfort, reconciles, serves, and witnesses to Christ, that is where the catechumens must be. And by having them walk with us as we do our work, the Body will feel challenged to be even more faithful to its mission. We learn that we are ever growing, offering and seeking forgiveness, learning to love and serve one another and those we all too easily call stranger.

Mission-Driven Catechumenate

If our catechumens are to be wherever the Body is, as our apprentice limbs and organs, then how might we keep this experience for both apprentice and experienced member more mission-oriented and mission-driven? We could look again at the four elements of catechumenal formation pointed out in the paragraph 75 of the Rite. As elaborated there so well and succinctly, these elements of formation are word, liturgy, community's life, and service/mission. What follows is hardly exhaustive, only suggestive of possibilities for mission centeredness in these elements of community life and catechumenal formation.

The Word

Is there anything more basic to our catechumens than the ministry of the Word that inflames and sustains all Christian life? This is the sacrament of the catechumenate. The cycles of lectionary readings for the Sunday Liturgy of the Word are permeated with the vision of God's hunger and longing for a world different from the one we inhabit. And this very longing resonates with everything that is deepest in the human heart. It is in this respect especially that humanity is made in God's image and likeness.

Does our Sunday preaching address this hunger, name it and elicit its full potential? Do our readers prepare each Sunday to proclaim the readings with hearts open to the Word speaking to them and to the community and world out of the fires of this restless, divine compassion? If we do not speak to the longing which God has placed in the human heart, no amount of religious education will ever make the difference.

The world is not as it should be, as God meant it to be. Our reading and preaching of God's Word must embrace the whole story of God's unrelenting pursuit of a people and world set right at last, in God's time and at God's expense. It is an expense and longing that Christ's Body is uniquely to em-Body. Can we let the Word in all its power name the lack we share with the world and that lack's great resolution in Christ? We must. We owe our catechumens, ourselves, and the very world we inhabit nothing less.

With this vision in mind, we must proclaim the story whole. This, if for no other reason, is why our catechumens are to be fed with a full round of at least one year of the cycle of Scriptures at Sunday liturgy. This is their right by virtue of being made members of the household of Christ when they were accepted into the catechumenate. And it is our responsibility to apprentice them under the Word for nothing less than a year. If we do so, issues of justice and charity that are on our doorstep will be named and addressed in ways uniquely suited to the individual and cultural realities of our communities of faith.

LITURGY

As Roman Catholics, we too often make "liturgy" synonymous with the Eucharist. We must do better. Eucharist is the centerpiece of the Church's liturgy, where it leads and that from which it flows. But the liturgy is so much more. It is the full panoply of hours, days, weeks, seasons, feasts, and sacramental gatherings that together make the liturgical year of Christians. It is the many ways in which we gather in public worship throughout the year as a whole that is the liturgy of the Church. And it is through the ministrations of this year that we are immersed in the whole of the paschal mystery of Jesus Christ as our very way of life. This liturgical year is a school of prayer, the place in which we learn how to stand in God's presence and worship. But what does this kind of language really mean?

One of my mentors in liturgy, Bob Hovda, was fond of saying that the liturgy is "kingdom play." It is an image to dwell on. In our liturgical gatherings we are about the mission of fashioning an alternative way of being in the world and for its salvation. This beloved creation of God's is not as it should be. The work of liturgy is to help restore it, in God's grace, to what it was always meant to be. And this work begins with Christ's Body learning together to be the embodied presence of Christ. In the liturgy we are learning and rehearsing the ways of the kingdom that God is fashioning among us. And this the world is longing and groaning to know.

Within this vision we see that in the cycle of liturgical assemblies throughout the year, especially the Eucharist, we bring all we are and the world we inhabit to be fashioned into the new world of the kingdom being prepared by God in Christ. Each time we assemble to worship the Lord, in the grace of the Lord's presence among us we carve out a different way of being. We need, then, to take our rituals to heart and to celebrate them conscientiously and robustly. By doing so, just consider the alternative ways of being in this world in which our catechumens will be formed. They will see a care, graciousness, and reverence for others, among them the stranger and those we do not know well. They will see time itself treated as a gift from the Creator, not to be taken for granted and certainly not to be rushed—time as the moment we have right now to do together what it is right and just to do before our God. Further, we explicitly acknowledge and raise up creation itself in our worship as "gift" and the "work of human hands." Through our worship we explicitly show the things of creation respect as a part of God's divine purpose, material being imperceptibly transformed into the stuff of the kingdom just as surely as we are.

COMMUNITY'S LIFE

The life of our communities of faith needs to attend to issues of maintenance but to be driven by issues of mission. Certainly the bills must be paid, the roof fixed, the plumbing leaks plugged, our sick visited, our young educated. But we do not have the luxury as Christ's Body of not being that Body for the larger communities of which we are a part. We take care of maintenance in order to be able to do the mission. We are fed at our eucharistic table in order to set the tables of others, especially those lacking anything to put on their tables.

If our catechumens do not encounter this vision and its practical results, we have not formed them in the way of life of Christ. We cannot authentically embody the ritual without also doing the work. And our catechumen-apprentices need to be intimately involved in that work with us.

What might they see, experience, and have a part in if our parishes see their lives as embodying mission? They might see a parish whose budget is subjected each year to fundamental and critical questions of how it is serving Christ's desires in the larger community. Can we, for example, continue to provide an education in our Catholic school primarily to middle- and upper-middle-class children? What witness does this give to the larger community, a number of whose children may be at risk either educationally or socially? The Catholic social principles of solidarity should cause us to pause, since all children are our children.

Do our catechumens see us actively supporting efforts in the larger community, not just our own efforts, to feed the hungry and to provide clothing and shelter to the homeless? Do they see us, individually and sometimes corporately, lending our voices and our vote to local, national, and international issues not only of charity, but of justice? These are issues that of their nature respond best to joint effort and long-term commitment.

MISSION/SERVICE

So much of what has already been said is related directly to our communities' awareness of and commitment to apostolic life and witness, to mission. If our vision, emerging from the ministry of the Word, formed by the liturgy, and embodied in our common life, is not one of mission, the very mission of Christ, then we are failing to experience the Word whole, to be authentically formed by our worship, and to challenge one another to faithful living. This is a central question for the effectiveness of the catechumenate. Remember that it is a whole way of life in which our apprentice members are being formed.

Do our catechumens see us encouraging one another to witness to our values in our homes, workplaces, and communities? Do they see us providing the practical means of support for this witness? Do they experience us actively seeking continual adult formation in our way of life, knowing that we can always know more deeply and do what we do better? Do they see that formation resulting in a resolute hunger to share Christ with others, in ways appropriate to them, with respectful listening being the first and most important step?

There is a great deal at stake in getting the recovery of the catechumenate right. It is all about evangelization, an evangelization of others and of ourselves in the process, an evangelization leading to transformation. We must continue to be challenged by the basic vision of the *Rite of Christian Initiation of Adults*. If the world is to change, we must first change. The stakes are immense. The world is going with us in some remarkable and unimaginable way to the kingdom that God is fashioning in our midst. The initiation process is helping us to relearn how to be the kind of people that we are called to be. The urgency of the task is God's, and now it must be ours.

John Roberto

Weaving Together
Liturgy, Justice, and Catechesis

> Catechesis is an essentially ecclesial act. The true subject of cate-
> chesis is the Church which, continuing the mission of Jesus the
> Master and, therefore animated by the Holy Spirit, is sent to be
> the teacher of the faith. The Church imitates the Mother of the
> Lord in treasuring the Gospel in her heart. She proclaims it,
> celebrates it, lives it, and she transmits it in catechesis to all
> those who have decided to follow Jesus Christ.[1]

The focus of this essay to explore practical ways to connect
liturgy and justice by proposing a model of Church-centered
faith formation that integrates liturgy, justice, *and* catechesis.
Much attention has been given to the difficulty of making practical, pastoral connections between the Church's liturgical life
and the work of justice. It is my belief that making this connection would be greatly enhanced by seeing catechesis as an
essential element in making the connection and in adopting a
more comprehensive approach to faith formation—one that
sees the Church as the "true subject of catechesis."

Let me illustrate this approach with a story. At St. Vincent de
Paul parish[2] the social justice coordinator and volunteer team

---

[1] *General Directory for Catechesis* (Washington, D.C.: USCC, 1997) n. 78.

[2] St. Vincent de Paul parish is a generalized description of the types
of things parishes are doing to move toward a Church-centered faith

are preparing for the annual, February parish-wide justice and service project. St. Vincent de Paul parish, together with four other congregations—three Protestant churches and a Jewish synagogue, provides shelter and food for the area's homeless throughout the month of February. St. Vincent de Paul parish is responsible for preparing evening meals for fifty to eighty people each day. It is a monumental organizing task, but this year something is different.

St. Vincent de Paul parish has made their February justice and service commitment a focus of their catechetical and liturgical ministries. The parish-wide focus for February is "House the Homeless; Feed the Hungry." The focusing Scripture reading is taken from the Lenten Lectionary—Isaiah, chapter 58: "share your bread with the hungry, and bring the homeless poor into your house" (v. 7) and "If you offer your food to the hungry and satisfy the needs of the afflicted, then your light shall rise in the darkness . . ." (v. 10).

The St. Vincent de Paul catechetical ministry has designed a variety of ways to prepare all ages and generations for their participation in "House the Homeless; Feed the Hungry" and then to engage them in preparing and serving one meal during the month. Catholic Social Teaching and the Lenten Lectionary readings will be a primary resource for preparation. The homilies during February will address the justice message in "House the Homeless; Feed the Hungry." A special justice focus will be given to the preparation of the Ash Wednesday liturgy and homily, drawing upon the themes of fasting and almsgiving. The music director has selected several songs that express musically the justice theme. These songs will be used in the catechetical programs, at home, and at Sunday worship.

During three sessions in January, all of the child catechetical programs focus on hunger and homelessness with each class assigned one meal to prepare and serve. The first session ex-

---

formation approach through the Center for Ministry Development's *Generations of Faith Project*. All of the examples in the story are actual parish activities. To learn more about the *Generations of Faith Project*, go to <www.generationsoffaith.org/> or <www.cmdnet.org/>.

plores the local and global situation of hunger and homeless through stories and a video presentation. The second session engages the children in reflecting on the message of justice and the call to act for justice and serve those in need, by exploring several focusing Scripture readings (e.g., Isaiah 58, Matthew 25) and the themes of Catholic Social Teaching (life and the dignity of the human person, rights and responsibilities, and option for the poor and vulnerable). The First Eucharist classes use their second session to explore the connections between Eucharist and justice. Parents join with their children for session three to learn about what their children are studying, to prepare for serving a meal during February, and to review how to use the special "House the Homeless; Feed the Hungry" Home Kit of activities and resources.

The focus for the middle-school and the high-school programs in January is also "House the Homeless; Feed the Hungry." Through a simulation game and video presentation, the young adolescents and older adolescents explore the reality and causes of hunger and homelessness in their community and around the world. They reflect on the scriptural teachings on justice and the major themes of Catholic Social Teaching, and examine a variety of ways to overcome hunger and homelessness through direct service and social change. Each group then organizes several meals that they will prepare and serve in February. In addition, the middle school youth produce a series of posters to promote "House the Homeless; Feed the Hungry" month, and the high-school youth organize a campaign to educate the entire parish and community about the needs of the homeless and what can be done.

All of the young adult and adult faith sharing groups dedicate several sessions in January and February to focus on "House the Homeless; Feed the Hungry" by reflecting on key scriptural passages and the Lenten Lectionary readings. Each small group selects one meal to prepare and serve. All of the parish committees, councils, and organizations that meet in January and February open their meetings with a special prayer service and video presentation on the "House the Homeless; Feed the Hungry" theme. Each organization is invited to prepare and serve a meal.

The catechetical ministry has also designed congregation-wide educational strategies, including a special bulletin insert for two weeks on the reality of hunger and homelessness and the scriptural and Church teachings on justice. The posters, developed by the young adolescents, are prominently displayed in all church gathering places.

The "House the Homeless; Feed the Hungry" Home Kit contains daily prayers for those in need, Lenten prayers and Scripture reflections on Catholic Social Teaching themes, a "bread-baking for the hungry" activity and ritual, learning activities to explore the issue and study selected Scripture passages, websites to visit (e.g., <www.povertyusa.org/>—the Catholic Campaign for Human Development's website), guidelines for preparing and serving a meal, an Operation Rice Bowl kit (from Catholic Relief Services), and ideas for almsgiving/service during Lent. Every home in the parish receives a kit.

St. Vincent de Paul Online, the parish's website, features an online version of the Home Kit; additional information, articles, and stories about hunger and homeless; and ideas for action, e.g., working with local and national organizations to alleviate hunger and homelessness. Individuals and families can also register online to prepare and serve a meal. For further exploration and action, links to specially selected websites are included. The parish website also provides a forum to share stories about individual and family service experiences during February and throughout Lent.

After each experience of serving a meal, individuals and families are guided in a reflection on their justice and service experience and its connection to the life of the Church and the Lenten season. They share their thoughts and feelings, and explore how to apply their learning in their daily lives as Catholics. The catechetical ministry provides a variety of ideas for living justice and service during Lent and throughout the year.

Wherever you go in the St. Vincent de Paul parish, people of all ages and generations are united in a common endeavor: to explore the Christian tradition of justice and service, to serve the needs of the hungry and homeless in their community and world, and to live the Gospel call to justice and service throughout the year.

Faith formation at St. Vincent de Paul is being transformed by an approach that is centered on the formative events of the church community and the participation of all ages and generations in the shared experiences of church life. This events-centered approach has the following important features:

- It is developed around the events in the life of the faith community: the Church year; sacraments and liturgy, prayer, justice and service, community life, and proclamation of the Word. It recognizes that the Church does not have an educational program; it *is* an educational program. *The Church is the curriculum.* As the quote from the *General Directory for Catechesis,* which opens this article, states, "Catechesis is an essentially ecclesial act. The true subject of catechesis is the Church. . . ."

- It is *emergent*—the beliefs and practices for living as a Catholic today are embedded in the life and events of the faith community. The catechetical task is to draw out from the life of the Church the "content" (themes, actions, practices), which becomes a focus for the faith formation curriculum for all ages and generations.

- It seamlessly weaves *home* and *parish* in a comprehensive model of faith formation that places an emphasis on programs, activities, and resources for nurturing faith growth at home—as individuals and families. It promotes family faith growth by empowering families to share, celebrate, and live the Catholic faith at home and in the world. It views the family as the church of the home, and a community of learning and practice.

- It emphasizes experiential learning in community. Participation in the events of church life is learning. The *General Directory for Catechesis* supports this communal view of learning. It speaks about catechesis as a "true school of the faith" and as "an initiation and apprenticeship in the entire Christian life." We learn by immersion into the life of the faith community. We learn by participating in the life of the faith community, especially by engaging in the practices of the faith community. We learn by studying, practicing, performing, and reflecting, but most importantly, we are engaged in *doing* the activity in the first place.

- It utilizes a catechetical process of *preparing* all ages and all generations for meaningful participation in church events through a variety of learning programs, *engaging* them in church events, and guiding them in *reflecting* and *applying* the significance and meaning of the events for their lives as Catholics. *Preparation* empowers people's participation in the event. It provides the activities and resources that help people to learn what they need to know and be able to do in order to participate fully in the event. Preparation programs and activities are designed to help people of all ages and generations develop, *know-how, know-what, know-why*. *Engagement* is the heart of the process—people are transformed by their experience and practice. We learn best by doing. The process comes full circle with *reflection* on the meanings people draw from their engagement and *application* of those insights to their daily life.

- It provides *alignment* of learning through common events and themes that are experienced and explored by all ages and all generations in the parish community. It provides a support system for learning in the parish and at home by focusing on common events and themes that engage the whole parish community. The fundamental unity of the parish and of faith formation is strengthened by establishing common events and themes that are explored by all members of the community at home and through parish faith formation programs.

This model of faith formation holds great promise for making justice and service "constitutive" of faith formation and for making the connection between justice and liturgy. It focuses our attention on how justice and service is already embedded in the life of the Church. The themes of Catholic Social Teaching are embedded in the Church year, the Lectionary, the celebration of the sacraments, and the community's actions of service. The motivation to serve those in need and act for justice is already embedded in the life of the Church. The primary task is to unearth the message and motivation so that it can become the focus of faith formation for all ages and generations.

Consider the possibilities that are already present in the life of a parish community each year. We find justice and service themes in the seasons of Advent and Lent: the Lectionary readings, parish service projects, the celebration of Las Posados in Advent, etc. We find justice and service themes in Church-year feasts and saints days: Pentecost, Corpus Christi, Christ the King (Cycle A), St. Francis and St. Clare, St. Vincent de Paul, St. Martin de Porres, Dorothy Day, Oscar Romero, and others. We find justice and service themes in the Sunday Lectionary: the feeding and banquet stories, the Sermon on the Mount and Sermon on the Plain, Matthew 25, the rich young man, the rich man and Lazarus, etc. We find justice and service themes in our calendar year events: Martin Luther King Jr.'s Birthday (January), Earth Day (April), World Food Day (October), Thanksgiving (November), and so on. We find justice and service in the national Catholic Church calendar: Respect Life Month, Mission Sunday, Migrant and Refugee Week, Catholic Campaign for Human Development, etc. We find a variety of service projects in our parish, and in local, diocesan, and national organizations around which we can organize faith formation.

Imagine a whole year of an events-centered curriculum for all ages and generations in the parish community that focuses on justice and service and makes connections to the major themes of Catholic Social Teaching.[3] Imagine the Sunday liturgies—rituals, homilies, music—also focused on the same themes as the catechetical program. Image a coordinated effort among liturgical, catechetical, and social justice leaders of the parish to make this plan a reality. Imagine parish preparation programs and reflection activities, as well as home activities for all ages, around the following events:

September: Labor Day
    Focus: Dignity of Work and Rights of Workers
    Engagement in the Labor Day weekend liturgy

---

[3] See United States Catholic Conference, *Sharing Catholic Social Teaching —Challenges and Directions* (Washington, D.C.: USCC, 2000).

October: Respect Life Month
>   Focus: Life and Dignity of the Human Person
>   Engagement in Sunday worship and justice and service actions on life issues

November: Thanksgiving—Feeding the Hungry
>   Focus: Rights and Responsibilities and Option for the Poor and Vulnerable
>   Engagement in the Thanksgiving liturgy and service projects focused on hunger

December: Los Posados—Shelter and Housing
>   Focus: Rights and Responsibilities and Option for the Poor and Vulnerable
>   Engagement in Los Posados, the Advent Liturgies, and service projects focused on shelter/housing

January: World Peace Day (January 1) and Martin Luther King Jr. Celebration
>   Focus: Peace and Nonviolence
>   Engagement in MLK celebrations and actions for peace

February and March: Lent—Living Justice (Isaiah 58)
>   Focus: Rights and Responsibilities and Option for the Poor and Vulnerable
>   Engagement in the liturgies, rituals, prayer, and service activities of Lent

April: Earth Day
>   Focus: Care for God's Creation
>   Engagement in environment action

May: Pentecost
>   Focus: Solidarity
>   Engagement in the Pentecost liturgy and actions that promote global solidarity and multicultural understanding

This is only one example of what is possible. Research the possibilities in your own parish community. Create your own plan for integrating liturgy, justice, and catechesis in a holistic approach to faith formation that involves all ages and generations. The opportunities are already present in your parish community!

Forming Youth for Justice and Worship

There is no such thing as apathy

A friend of mine, Tom, agreed to provide a retreat weekend for high-school juniors and seniors at a parish on the coast of Northern California. The focus of the retreat was Catholic social teachings. Tom showed up with presentations planned, prayer services prepared, charts in hand, and group discussions ready to go. As the retreat got underway, it became clear that Tom's plan was going nowhere. The retreat leaders apologized to him for the students' apathy and indicated that the youth really did not want to be there but were attending to fulfill a requirement for their confirmation program. Tom put the plans for the retreat aside, sat down on the floor, and talked to the youth. They asked him, "What's all this justice stuff about anyway? What does it have to do with *our* lives?" He listened to their questions and then asked them about what was going on in their lives and in their community. One young man got pretty stirred up as he told the group about the situation at the local beach. He said he was no longer allowed to go to the beach, because medical waste kept coming ashore and contaminating the whole area. Many students commented about how unfair and disgusting the situation at the beach was. Tom suggested a visit to the beach, so off they went. They walked around the restricted area and looked at the ruins of their beach. Tom asked the students to talk about what they saw and felt. They were not apathetic any longer.

The students spoke with passion. They were confused, sad, and angry about what they saw at the beach. Tom listened and asked them to analyze the situation. He then shared scriptural passages and social teachings that concerned the reverence, care, and stewardship of the earth. The group took time to pray, and at Mass that evening, their experience at the beach was at the horizon of their prayers as they joined in worship.

The next morning, Tom asked the students what they wanted to do in response to what they experienced at the beach. At first they were confused and wondered what they could do. Tom reminded them of the steps they had already taken and told them that the last step was to take action. Since they could not get directly involved in the cleanup of the beach, the most obvious action was advocacy. They chose two youth to attend an upcoming public hearing about the beach and wrote letters to legislators, the press, and people in the medical industry. Following the retreat, Tom commented to me, "There is no such thing as apathy. We just have to find where each person's passion lies."

Many people assume that youth are apathetic. Youth are also often portrayed as being self-centered, materialistic, and shallow. However, a recent study of the current generation of adolescents reveals a very different picture. In fact, youth are far from apathetic. Most youth believe in God and participate in weekly worship. Many youth participate in regular service for others. In fact, youth have a higher percentage of weekly worship attendance and service participation than any other age group.[1]

The question of how we can form youth for justice and liturgy might seem overwhelming at first. Indeed, forming youth for justice and worship is challenging, but half the challenge is for the adults in the community. Adults need to sit on the floor and talk to youth. Adults need to listen. They need to find out what youth are passionate about and then, like Jesus on the road to Emmaus, help connect life stories with the treasure of faith that has been entrusted to all of us.

---

[1] George H. Gallup, Jr., *The Spiritual Life of Young Americans: Approaching the Year 2000* (Princeton, N.J.: George H. Gallup International Institute, 1999) 3 and 10.

The Hungers of Youth

To form youth for justice and worship, the most basic hungers of young people need to be addressed. One such hunger that goes to the heart of our efforts is the longing youth have to be part of the community of disciples. As disciples, we serve those in need in Jesus' name and celebrate our relationship to God with engaging and transforming worship. Youth want to be part of the Church, the "community of ministers to the kingdom."[2] Youth hunger to belong, but they also want to be essential to the Church community.

At a recent workshop, I asked young people what they needed to participate more fully in their parish liturgy. I expected the usual answers—youthful music, dynamic homilies, more involvement of youth in ministries. However, one young woman stated clearly her primary need: "What I need is to know that someone would notice if I wasn't there." She spoke a truth about youth involvement. Youth are essential to the commitments they make to their schools, workplaces, and homes. They want to be essential to the Church community as we pray, share our lives, and serve others in God's name. Many adults assume that youth are only interested in peer relationships. This assumption does not bear out in studies, nor in conversations with young people. Youth need opportunities to be with peers, but they crave acceptance in the community at large. They want to know that they belong in all of the communities that they are part of: family, school, city or town, circles of friends, and church.

Young people want to be essential in the Church, they also want to be important in the world of which they are a part. They want to make a difference, stretch their wings and exercise their talents and gifts. Adolescence is a time when youth become more aware of their capacities. They learn what they are good at doing and what they are not. They are looking for a place to put all of their idealism and a way to pour out their pent up energy and creativity. As the United States Catholic

[2] Thomas O'Meara, *A Theology of Ministry* (Ramsey, N.J.: Paulist Press, 1983) 30.

Bishops state in *Renewing the Vision—A Framework for Catholic Youth Ministry,* "If we are to succeed, we must offer young people a spiritually challenging and world-shaping vision that meets their hunger for the chance to participate in a worthy adventure."[3]

Another important aspect of adolescence is that searching and inner growth are predominate during this stage of development. Adolescents are aware that they are growing, and they often feel caught between childhood expectations and adult responsibilities. In the midst of this, they "try on" behaviors, attitudes, and activities, much like the way they try on clothes in a store. They wonder, "What do I look like wearing this? Does this feel like me?" Youth know they need room to grow, but they also need safe boundaries to bounce up against.

The hungers of youth include a hunger for community, adventure, and a safe place to grow, all of which are interconnected. Our response to youth must be related to these same hungers. In ministering to youth, these hungers present an opportunity to promote discipleship by encouraging meaningful participation in the worship and life of the community of disciples, giving them a safe place to question, learn and grow, and empowering them to serve others. These three actions, which are rooted in worship and justice, are key to our ministry to youth.

The challenges and opportunities noted above are at the heart of the vision for youth ministry. In *Renewing the Vision,* the U.S. Catholic bishops lay out three goals for youth ministry that match the hungers for adventure, connection, and a safe place to grow:

Goal 1: To empower young people to live as disciples of Jesus Christ in our world today.

Goal 2: To draw young people to responsible participation in the life, mission, and work of the Catholic faith community.

Goal 3: To foster the total personal and spiritual growth of each young person.[4]

---

[3] NCCB, *Renewing the Vision—A Framework for Catholic Youth Ministry* (Washington, D.C.: USCC, 1997) 10.

[4] Ibid., 9, 11 and 15.

Our ministries of justice and worship must work hand in hand to accomplish these goals. Both justice and worship are integral to discipleship. By connecting worship with active service, we strive for wholeness as disciples and avoid many of the pitfalls that can accompany an unbalanced spirituality. Both justice and worship help youth to participate more fully in the faith community. After all, one of the best ways to get to know someone is to work, play, and pray together. Moreover, worship and service provide youth with opportunities for personal and spiritual growth by challenging them and giving them a place to share their gifts.

Everything Connects

The relationship between justice and worship is important to all members of the faith community, but for youth this relationship becomes a litmus test of relevancy. They look to a community that serves as Jesus Christ did and celebrates the relationship with their loving God through vibrant worship. Connecting our ministry of justice to our worship provides youth with many avenues to address their hungers for community, growth, and adventure. Further, justice and worship connect with the idealism that accompanies adolescence. Youth have a heightened sense of hypocrisy, and they will use their radar to spot inconsistencies, especially in adults who are closest to them. This ability of youth is not always comfortable for parents, youth workers, and teachers, but it is a wonderful glimpse into the idealistic vision of the world many young people hold.

Worship and the work of justice offer wonderful ways for youth and the adult members of the community to connect. Twenty years ago, youth ministry was much more focused on creating a community of youth. To address youth's call to service, special programs and opportunities were created for youth to serve with each other. In a similar way, the challenge of helping youth to participate in the liturgy was often met by creative prayer services for youth or by creating special "youth" liturgies that addressed the needs of youth as something separate and apart from the whole congregation. There is a time and a place for youth to work in service and worship with their peers; however, many youth leaders and faith communities today see the need to include youth more intentionally in the wider assembly. This is an important directive of *Renewing the Vision*, which calls for parishes to be "a place where [young people] are welcome, grow in Jesus Christ, and minister side by side with the adults of the community."⁵

The need to include youth in the broader faith community is also noted in mainline youth ministry publications. For instance, Kenda Creasy Dean critiques the separate youth congregation approach in *The Godbearing Life—The Art of Soul Tending for Youth Ministry*. She describes this approach as "the one-eared Mickey Mouse model of youth ministry."⁶ In this model, the congregation as a whole (visualized as a large circle) has an attached but separate youth congregation (visualized as a smaller attached circle). Youth experience belonging, worship, and service as part of a youth congregation that runs parallel with the adult congregation. At the end of years of participation in a youth congregation, a young person may never make the transition into the adult congregation because it is foreign to him or her. Youth find a level of energy, style of worship, and network of relationships for which years of youth ministry have not prepared them. As Kenda Creasy Dean states:

> The upshot of the overwhelming dominance of youth-group models of ministry was a deepening chasm between youth ministry and the theology of the church as a whole. When youth graduated from the "youth group"—the only form of ministry many young people had ever experienced—they effectively graduated from church as well.⁷

To avoid "parallel congregations," attention should be given to the youth within the context of the broader congregation, even if at the same time, they are ministered to within their

---

⁵ Ibid., 13.

⁶ Kenda Creasy Dean and Ron Foster, *The Godbearing Life—The Art of Soul-Tending for Youth Ministry* (Nashville: Upper Room Books, 1998) 31.

⁷ Ibid., 30.

own peer group. In the ministry of justice, this means youth and adults participate together in opportunities to learn about justice and serve those in need. In worship, this means that the full, conscious, and active participation of youth *and* adults is fostered in every liturgy.

Another area of growth in youth ministry is the increased emphasis on empowering youth for discipleship. Service, ministry, and leadership have always been important components of youth ministry, but many leaders are feeling the urgency to place active discipleship at the core of youth ministry efforts. This urgency is not universally felt; in many communities, adolescence is seen more as a time of waiting and preparing. Youth are given the information and experiences needed to be adult members of the community. Youth are often told that they are "the future of the Church"; however, this approach does not match the reality of adolescence. Youth are looking for a place that will hold their energy and enthusiasm *now*. They are searching for an energizing vision and a passionate, active community. They are the future of the Church, but they are already the young Church of today. In *Starting Right—Thinking Theologically about Youth Ministry*, Kenda Creasy Dean explains:

> If youth ministry is going to help adolescents become practical theologians, then we must begin by helping them practice faith, which requires both a relationship with Jesus Christ and opportunities for ministry as teenagers. Youth Ministry that emphasizes evangelism, without simultaneously giving adolescent opportunities to serve in substantive ministry, eviscerates discipleship. Youth Ministry that seeks Christian action with a growing relationship with Jesus reduces it to good works. Neither dimension can stand on its own as faith.[8]

It's All About Discipleship

An important way to engage youth and the whole community in vibrant worship is by continuing to strengthen the relation-

[8] Kenda Creasy Dean, ed., *Starting Right—Thinking Theologically about Youth Ministry* (Grand Rapids, Mich.: Zondervan Publishing House, 2001) 33.

ship between liturgy and justice in communal celebrations. This is not an additional layer or theme that we impose, but rather, it is allowing the true nature of liturgy to emerge. The Scriptures, prayers, and hymns of our shared prayer cry out for justice. Attention to the poor and those in need is remembered through our homilies, the prayers of the faithful, and our continued service following the dismissal. As a community, if we bridge the chasm between justice and worship in the community, everyone, including our youth, will be formed for discipleship.

How do we form youth for justice and worship? We take the time to learn about young people. We learn about their passions, their concerns, and their dreams. We learn about their interests and gifts. We take the time to build up the relationships between youth, adults, and children in the community. We form youth for justice and worship throughout all of our ministries with youth. We intentionally strive to connect discipleship and faith with the everyday life of today's youth. Youth will be inspired by the active service and authentic worship they see in lives of faith in the community. Youth will also inspire the community, as they bring their new energy, ideas, and creativity to the gap between the world as we know it and the kingdom that Jesus described. Youth and adults will build each other up in justice and worship. It's all about discipleship, just as it has been since the days of the earliest Christians:

> Awe came upon everyone, because many wonders and signs were being done by the apostles. All who believed were together and had all things in common; they would sell their possessions and goods and distribute the proceeds to all, as any had need. Day by day, as they spent much time together in the temple, they broke bread at home and ate their food with glad and generous hearts, praising God and having the goodwill of all the people. And day by day the Lord added to their number those who were being saved (Acts 2:43-47).[9]

[9] *The Catholic Youth Bible: New Revised Standard Version* (Winona, Minn.: St. Mary's Press, 2000).

Suggestions for Forming Youth for Justice and Worship

The following suggestions provide practical illustrations of how youth can be formed for justice and worship.

- Connect youth with mentors who demonstrate an integrated spirituality of worship and justice. For instance, include a ministry and service mentorship within confirmation preparation for adolescents. Select and prepare mentors for liturgical ministries and service ministries; assign pairs of mentors with a pair of youth. Provide opportunities for learning, participation in ministry, reflection, and prayer.

- Encourage awareness among youth about justice issues today and involve youth in praying for peace and justice. One possibility is to invite youth to create a "Peace Prayer Candle," by having them select articles and pictures from newspapers/news magazines that represent areas of the world and people to pray with and for. Attach the pictures and a collage of the headlines to a large votive candle. Provide a prayer to help youth pray when they light the candle. Another possibility is to involve youth in preparing prayers of the faithful. Invite a group of youth to reflect on the readings for Sunday liturgy and the context of what is happening in the community and world today. Have youth compose prayers that link worship with justice and action.

- Utilize Scripture as a way help youth see the relationship between faith, worship, and justice. Use a *lectio divina* process to prepare youth for justice involvements and participation in liturgy.

- Prepare for and conclude justice/service involvements within the context of liturgy. Include prayer in each element of justice education and service involvement. For instance, conclude a weekend service project with the celebration of the Eucharist.

- Relate personal and corporate morality to experiences of liturgy.

- Reflect on the relationship between faith, worship, and justice throughout the liturgical and calendar year.

Resources

FORMING YOUTH FOR LITURGY

The National Federation for Catholic Youth Ministry. *From Age to Age: The Challenge of Worship with Adolescents.* Winona, Minn.: St. Mary's Press, 1997.

Celebrating the Lectionary. San Jose, Calif.: Resource Publications, Inc., 1999.

Vibrant Worship. Winona, Minn.: St. Mary's Press, 2000.

Richstatter, Thomas. *Liturgy and Worship—A Course on Prayer and Sacraments.* New York: William H. Sadlier, Inc., 1998.

FORMING YOUTH FOR JUSTICE

Benson, Peter and Eugene C. Roehlkepartain. *Beyond Leaf Raking: Learning to Serve, Serving to Learn.* Nashville: Abingdon Press, 1993.

Bright, Thomas. *Poverty: Do it Justice!* New Rochelle, N.Y.: DBM, 1990. (A publication of the Center for Ministry Development.)

Bright, Thomas and John Roberto. *Human Rights: Do it Justice!* New Rochelle, N.Y.: DBM, 1990. (A publication of the Center for Ministry Development.)

O'Connell, Frances Hunt. *Giving and Growing: A Student's Guide for Service Projects.* Winona, Minn.: St. Mary's Press, 1990.

Salzman, Marian, et. al. *150 Ways Teens Can Make a Difference.* Princeton, N.J.: Peterson's Guides, 1991.

Godfrey Mullen, O.S.B.

Milling the Wheat, Crushing the Grapes: Justice in Liturgical Preparation[1]

Liturgical preparation is serious, holy, and important, because it is a work of justice.[2] None of us would want to be sent away as we approach with our gift that could lead us to settle our differences with a sister or brother. None of us would be interested in being pushed away because we're not worthy to worship, to celebrate, to receive. No, we enter the celebration prepared for the extraordinary experience of God's presence in the ordinary, in flat bread and sweet wine, in water and oil, in fire and wood. With all creation we enter the celebration to give praise, to give thanks.[3]

Liturgical preparation is an awesome task. Integrating the planning of liturgy with an eye to justice requires more than

---

[1] This paper presumes an understanding of justice as right relationship, based on the work of Mark Searle, "Serving the Lord with Justice," *Liturgy and Social Justice,* ed. Mark Searle (Collegeville: The Liturgical Press, 1980) 13–35. The author gratefully acknowledges the assistance of Sister Celine Hendley, O.S.B., and Sister Doris Nolte, O.S.B.

[2] See GIRM 5: "There must be the utmost care therefore to choose and to make wise use of those forms and elements provided by the Church, that in view of the circumstances of the people and the place, will best foster active and full participation and serve the spiritual well-being of the faithful."

[3] See GIRM 24.

the occasional singing of Joe Mattingly's "On That Holy Mountain" or David Haas' "We Are Called," as formative and helpful as these songs are. Patching over a well-planned liturgy with a well-intended "theme" of justice is sloppy at best and harmful at worst. Liturgical preparation itself must be an act of justice. Then, as the texts of the liturgy are proclaimed, it will be clear and authentic that what is being done is the fruit of justice.[4] Done well, liturgical preparation itself is communion. It is proclamation. It is reconciliation.

Liturgical Preparation Is Communion

The Tasks. Do liturgy committees acknowledge unity with the assembly when preparing liturgy? The awesome task should be carried out, first and foremost, with the assembly in mind. Because it is preparation of communal worship, it is certainly done *for* the community. We choose music the assembly can sing, craft a homily the assembly can and wants to comprehend, study the texts that will call the assembly to prayer, arrange an environment that allows the assembly to feel welcome. These are tasks we do for the well-being and sanctification of our sisters and brothers in Christ.

We choose music the assembly can sing in order that full-throated voices might support one another, might together in one voice create a majestic melody of praise.[5] We choose music the assembly can sing that expresses our deepest desires, our greatest hopes, our most closely guarded hurts. Such music gives an assembly voice in God's words to proclaim God's goodness, consolation, forgiveness, and peace. Music for worship stirs the depths of soul and heart. We choose music the assembly can sing naturally, authentically, and readily.

---

[4] See MCW 11: "The power of a liturgical celebration to share faith will frequently depend upon its unity—a unity drawn from the liturgical feast or season or from the readings appointed in the Lectionary as well as artistic unity flowing from the skillful and sensitive selection of options, music, and related arts."

[5] MCW 15: "The music used should be within the competence of most of the worshipers. It should suit their age-level, cultural background, and level of faith."

We craft homilies that are comprehensible to the assembly. Homilies arise from and for that great commingling of human experience and eternal beauty. Good preaching enhances an assembly's ability to understand and draws a whole assembly into fuller, more conscious, more active participation,[6] not only in those six to eight minutes, but in the whole celebration. Homilies speak to people about God's great deeds for us. Homilies must never be obtuse, pointless, aimless, unprepared, or lethal. Justice (right relationship) demands that they be practical and poetic, motivating and moving, human and humane.

Countless generations have experienced, shared, interpreted, and understood the Word that is always changing in its incarnation in the lives of its members. As the Church's members have grown, changed, developed, and spread, the neverchanging truth of God's Word and God's love incarnate continue to dwell among us. The Word takes flesh *in us* when psalms of lament become our own anguished cries to God. The Word takes flesh *in us* when the songs of praise in the book of Revelation become our hymns telling of God's glory.[7] The Word takes flesh *in us* when we allow ourselves to be molded by its demands. In preparing for liturgy, we provide the setting wherein faithful people encounter the eternal Word anew. The texts of readings, petitions, and prayers ought to evoke *some* response. If not, perhaps we have allowed the Word to grow weak, tepid, and powerless. Whether stories of jubilation or woe, triumph or defeat, tenderness or devastation, the Word of

[6] NCCB, *Fulfilled in Your Hearing: The Homily in the Sunday Assembly* (Washington, D.C.: USCC, 1982) 67: "Whatever its form, the function of the Eucharistic homily is to enable people to lift up their hearts, to praise and thank the Lord for his presence in their lives. It will do this more effectively if the language it uses is specific, graphic, and imaginative. The more we can turn to the picture language of the poet and the storyteller, the more we will be able to preach in a way that invites people to respond from the heart as well as the mind."

[7] See SC 84: "When this wonderful song of praise is worthily rendered . . . then it is truly the voice of the bride addressing her bridegroom; it is the very prayer which Christ himself, together with His body, addresses to the Father."

God is meant to shake us loose from our comfortable perches, to work for justice, to *help* bring about the kingdom of right- eousness, harmony, and right relationship. The texts of the Church's worship must draw the community to prayer. "More is required than the mere observance of the laws governing valid and licit celebrations" (SC 11). Carelessly reading liturgi- cal texts is not sufficient. The texts must come alive in the minds of the planners like the recollection of tasty food or the memory of a long-forgotten love. Not only should readings be *proclaimed* in the liturgy, the liturgy ought to proclaim the read- ings—the texts of God's living Word. Music, preaching, and reading must all be worthy proclamation of the Word that "promote[s] that warm and living love for scripture" (SC 24).

Like a guestroom, so a space of worship should be inviting and welcoming, but not too comfortable. The house of worship ought to be so arranged and built that the members of Christ's Body can gather together.[8] All should feel welcome, greeted by sisters and brothers glad at their meeting. Can the assembly readily and clearly experience itself as celebrating and giving thanks? Do we see ourselves *together* as the "subject of the liturgy?" Can we and do we approach the bountiful table to eat and drink our way to salvation? Is God's banquet spread for us our regular approach to the throne of justice and mercy? The space ought to be a welcoming environment, expressing the heritage and flavor of a community, but not too comfortable. Liturgy is formal. More important, liturgy sends a people forth to proclaim the justice, mercy, and compassion of God. Should our places of worship not spur us on to such proclamation? Does the liturgy not awaken within us an urgency to work toward that justice that set the world aright? "We are taught that God is preparing a new dwelling place and a new earth where justice will abide, and whose blessedness will answer and surpass all the longings for peace which spring up in the human heart" (GS 39). Good liturgy ought to be a haven of justice, but it must also be nourishment for the work of justice

[8] See references to the need for accessibility in NCCB, *Built of Living Stones: Art, Architecture, and Worship* (Washington, D.C.: USCC, 2000), es- pecially nos. 59, 61, 74, 86, 105, 109, and 211–14.

beyond the place of worship, a leaven for the "regeneration of society."[9] Our liturgical environment must be such that all God's people—the powerful and powerless, the mighty and meek—experience being drawn in and sent out. If a place is not comfortable enough, then the assembly will not feel welcome. If it is too comfortable, it is too tempting to stay put and avoid the work of proclamation to the ends of the earth. Such a balance is not always easy to achieve but necessary to pursue.

Liturgical preparation done *for* the community makes great demands. Let us be completely conscious of the fact that the way liturgy is prepared forms a community, molds it and shapes it. So then, let us ask some questions.

The Questions. Can the community sing the music we choose? Is the music *worthy* of our assembly's singing? Does the variety of our music give voice to individual and communal experience? Does what we sing plant God's Word in people's minds and hearts in such a way that we remember it? Do we give credit to composers and publishers so that they are rewarded justly for their work? Are ministers of music treated humanely for their generosity and held accountable for their serious task?

Are homilies well prepared? Does the homily make God's Word clearer? Does the homily address the entire assembly? Is the homily creative and interesting? Does the homily faithfully interpret the challenging Word of God? Is the assembly receiving a piece of art, both beautiful and eloquent? Can the homilist include *pertinent* current events to help the assembly apply God's Word in our own day? Should homilists refer to political situations or avoid them altogether?

Is the reader ready to *proclaim* the Word for the edification of the hearers? Do introductions, penitential rites, petitions, and announcements use language that is appropriate and inclusive? When easily misinterpreted pericopes are used, is some explanation or catechesis or interpretation given? Does the

---

[9] This understanding of liturgy as the basis for social regeneration owes its origins to Virgil Michel and others who were leaders in the United States' liturgical movement in the early- and middle-twentieth century. See, e.g., Virgil Michel, "The Liturgy: The Basis of Social Regeneration," *Orate Fratres* 9 (1935) 536–45.

approved translation of prayers, readings, and other texts express the usage and meaning in a particular culture? Is the sound system adequate so that even those who are hearing-impaired might hear God's Word? Is the ambo so designed that people of all heights might be able to proclaim the Word?

Is the space constructed and arranged to accommodate people with limited mobility? Does the environment invite the timid and powerless? Is the art representative of the culture of the assembly? Does the space need an assembly in order to be complete? Do decorations enhance or detract from noble simplicity? Do they assist or inhibit worship and access? Can one readily see that everyone gathered, each with a particular role, is part of the whole assembly?

Ministry by the Assembly. Liturgical preparation is communion, done in harmony with the assembly and *for* the assembly. But it is also a ministry done *by* the assembly. Liturgical ministers plan and prepare *within* a community. Then the work of the liturgy committee is more than representative; it is actually the work of the community. The community gathers to pray and sing, making Christ truly present (SC 7) during the celebration. And the community itself has done the preparation.

Preparation *by* the community requires the ministers involved to be one with the community. Being set apart—or worse, setting oneself apart—typically disqualifies one from being an effective liturgical minister or planner. Justice is right relationship and the right relationship of any liturgical minister is unity with the assembly—the assembly that has called these to ministry. Histrionics and quirks seldom make for good liturgical preparation. Pedestals (and stages) are easier to fall off than to stay on.

Preparation *by* the community requires a unity of mind and heart, along with some degree of common experience. The words of Ildefons Herwegen are instructive:

> Liturgical prayer life cannot be for (the priest) but one among many means of personal perfection. Rather it must be the unifying principle of his personality as a priest. All the petitions of the community find a place in his life of prayer and sacrifice. Consequently, everything in him organically and solely tends

toward awakening and fostering the divine life in the Mystical Body of Christ through light with the Church and, as its guide, in letting it flow upon the members of the community united with him by his word, which now no longer is a learned discourse or an academic teaching, but *life* drawn from the life of Christ.[10]

While referring to priest-presiders, this wisdom applies to all liturgical ministers in our day. Liturgical ministers wisely draw deeply from the well of life encountered within the assembly.

Liturgical ministers who do not count themselves among the assembly might help create a deep chasm between the "knowledgeable" and the "ignorant huddled masses." Such an outside view enables dual tracks to form in such a way that irrelevance results. It can eventuate an unreal view of the assembly and its abilities. Nothing is more dissonant with the Christian liturgy. Therefore, the vocation of the liturgical minister is one of service to the Christian assembly. The Second Vatican Council's Decree on Priestly Formation *(Optatam Totius)* insists that "seminarians should understand very plainly that they are called not to domination or to honors, but to give themselves over entirely to God's service and the pastoral ministry" (9). If this is the case for seminarians, ought it not be so for *all* liturgical ministers?

Liturgical preparation then is ministry for the community and by the community. Are liturgical ministers, both before and during the celebration, clearly members of the assembly? Does the planning of liturgy seek that balance of being authentically the community's own while pulling on toward growth and justice? Is the assembly clearly the subject of the liturgy? Does liturgical planning embody principles of justice directly and indirectly? Do the members of the assembly see right relationship modeled in their midst?

Each member of the assembly should feel some rightful place at the liturgical celebration because of how it has been planned and how it unfolds. Members of the assembly ought to prepare

---

[10] Ildefons Herwegen, "Liturgy and Preaching," *Orate Fratres* 7 (1932) 25–26.

themselves to receive and live God's Word,[11] to be ready and anxious to sing praise to God, to be affirmed and challenged by artistic homilies, and to be welcomed and sent from the place of prayer. Our own dispositions must be adjusted for the work at hand so that participation might be truly "knowing, active, and fruitful" (SC 11).

Liturgical Preparation Is Proclamation

Liturgical preparation is *proclamation* insofar as it sets out to enhance and vivify the presence of God's Word in the act of worship. It prepares a people to proclaim, interpret, and appropriate God's eternal Word—active, alive, real, and present in the proclaiming.[12] Pope John Paul II wrote, "[Christ the Teacher]'s words, his parables and his arguments are never separable from his life and his very being" (*Catechesi Tradendae* 9). To proclaim the Word of God is to proclaim justice, right relationship for all creation. Is this not food for the hungry, refreshment for the thirsty, rest for the oppressed, freedom for captives, shelter for the homeless, respect for the powerless, and a voice for the silenced?

Liturgy and its preparation proclaim food for the hungry. While we eat fairly well (as the dirty dishes tell), there are far too many in the world, in countries far away, in our own country, our own cities and neighborhoods, who live and die in hunger. They *remember* the food they last savored. These hungry must know profound gratitude when they are able to eat. The liturgy and its preparation proclaim food to the hungry. For in the meager meal of wheat wafer and wine become body and blood, the hungry are filled to fullness. The *Catechism of the Catholic Church* (1397) says that the Eucharist is for the poor. We are the poor, those in need of the Bread of Life. If the Body of Christ is given to us in fullness, how can we as its members not see *in ourselves* the bread for the life of the world? We are to be food

---

[11] See *Introduction to the Lectionary for Mass*, 47: All the faithful without exception must therefore always be ready to listen gladly to God's Word.

[12] See *Introduction to the Lectionary for Mass*, 44: "Christ's word gathers the people of God as one and increases and sustains them."

for the hungry! Do we count ourselves wheat milled and bread broken for the sustenance of the hungry? How have the hungry laid claim not only to our surplus, but to our very selves?

Liturgy and its preparation proclaim refreshment for the thirsty. Thirst affects our bodies quickly and when dehydrated, we are not ourselves. We need water in order for the body to purify itself of toxins. In most places, water is readily available; yet, there are those places where inhabitants are still "parched as burnt clay" (Ps 22). All around us, there are those who thirst for the mercy of forgiveness, for understanding and wisdom. The thirsty are here; we thirst for justice. In the liturgy, water becomes spirited water, living water, the wine of new hope. In Christ's compassion, water became wine. In Christ's glory, wine becomes the Blood of redemption. In liturgy and in its preparation, we become the wine in that cup, we are the grapes —squeezed, crushed, spirited, poured out. We are meant to be life for the thirsty.

Liturgy and its preparation proclaim rest to the oppressed. Anyone in the field of liturgy knows what it is to need rest. And some know all too well what it is to be oppressed, to be persecuted, to be out-maneuvered, to be out-powered in relationships that are not at all fair. Some in the world know oppression that passes quickly; others know it as a way of life—or a way of death. Oppression is being held in poverty. Catherine DeHueck Doherty wrote in 1938:

> Christ walks the earth in his poor. . . . In the liturgy we learn to know Christ. And if we truly know him, we shall recognize him everywhere, but especially in his poor, and we shall set our faces toward liberation of him from the yoke of injustice and pain, helping to bring about the reign of Christ the King in this world. And with it order, peace, and love, so that we shall be able to say: "I saw Christ today, and he was smiling."[13]

We are chided by the liturgy to give rightful rest to those we oppress.

Preparation and celebration of liturgy proclaim freedom to captives. People are held captive by death or fear, phobias and lack of

---

[13] "I Saw Christ Today." *Orate Fratres* 12 (1938) 309–10.

courage. Some are imprisoned in darkness and the shadow of death, and are held captive by addiction and self-destruction. Christ came to proclaim liberty to captives, freedom and release. Our task is to proclaim this very freedom that triumphed over death and darkness. No stone, no guard, not even death itself could contain life. Captives must die to destructive ways in order to experience this freedom. In prisons or on mountaintops, those who have died in destruction rise to the freedom given by truth, hope, and justice. Like wheat that is ground and grapes that are crushed, human disorder can die and captivity can be overcome, in order that life, glory, and right relationship result.

Christian communal worship and all that leads to it proclaim shelter to the homeless. Like sheep without a shepherd, people wandering in a desert, apostles without their messiah, the homeless wander the earth without place. Lost in familiar surroundings, the homeless clothe themselves so often in the wrappings of trash—bags designed for refuse. If they have not known their goodness as God's beloved creation, then we have failed, and they lay claim to our comfort and homes and tables and showers and warmth. Like Joseph and Mary in search of a room, like Moses afloat in the river, these sisters and brothers of ours deserve, need, and require shelter. How do we make the provisions? How do we house the wanderers among us?

The proclamation of respect for the powerless is the work of the Christian assembly. That each one has and takes a rightful place at liturgy proclaims that respect for each one. But what about those who have been so stripped of power that they are not able to present themselves? What about those who are counted weak and pathetic by the powerful? In the Eucharist all receive the same morsel, the same sip. The powerful and the weak receive the same portion, each empowered for living. But to the hungry, the poor, and the powerless, the meager portion *is* their power, their hope, their glory. Not given in pity, but with respect, the Body and Blood of Christ, whole and entire, is offered and taken in reverence. At Eucharist, in the liturgy, all are empowered to hear, to receive, to go forth proclaiming the wonders of *God's* justice.

Liturgy proclaims a voice to the silenced. Every human being is given a voice with which the praise of God is sung. Can being rendered voiceless by a power greater than oneself be the least bit humane? What about those who are rendered mute regarding their own healthcare, their own living conditions, or the direction of a government that theoretically represents them? The human voice is a gift from God, given for conversation and praise. Liturgy is that arena where every believer has a voice for praise, talented musicians and the tone-deaf alike.

Fundamentally, the preparation and celebration of liturgy proclaims *hospitality*. It proclaims that place where we are fed and refreshed, where we are given space to relax and be free, where we take shelter and speak what we believe, where we are hallowed for who we are and respected as God's beloved. Good liturgy welcomes and then sends out like good hospitality.

Liturgical Preparation Is Reconciliation

"So when you are offering your gift at the altar, if you remember that your brother or sister has something against you, leave your gift there before the altar and go; first be reconciled to your brother or sister, and then come and offer your gift" (NRSV Matt 5:23-24). The celebration of liturgy requires our mindfulness of hospitality for the world's needy while it clings to preparation as reconciliation. Without the reconciliation of sisters and brothers, we have no hope for the liturgy to work justice. If reconciliation (the *restoration* of right relationship) does not take place in preparation, then can the sign of peace be authentic? Do we have any hope for that perfect offering from East to West? Reconciliation is the result of liturgy; it is the way to liturgy.

Narrow, isolationist, individualistic vision among liturgical planners, ministers, and assemblies call for reconciliation. If ground wheat is intended to be one loaf and crushed grapes one cup, then we who are grains of wheat and luscious grapes are intended for such oneness as well. Does liturgical preparation seek to know the needs of all the members of the community? Do planners seek to understand the viewpoint of the disgruntled community member? Does the group work in *conjunction* or in *opposition* to other groups in the community? Do we strive to articulate together the vision of our communal worship? Are our ministers recognized for the talents they share and the efforts they make? Are paid liturgical ministers given a just and competitive wage? Does all our liturgical preparation flow from a fundament of our being grains of wheat milled and clumps of grapes crushed that we and all the world eat and drink to our salvation through Jesus Christ the Lord?

> It is the goal of this most sacred Council to intensify the daily growth of Catholics in Christian living; to make more responsive to the requirements of our times those Church observances which are open to adaptation; to nurture whatever can contribute to the unity of all who believe in Christ; and to strengthen those aspects of the Church which can help summon all humanity into its embrace. Hence the Council has special reasons for judging it a *duty* to provide for the renewal and fostering of the liturgy (SC 1).

The renewal of the liturgy focuses on the growth of Christian living, growth in justice and in peace, the interweaving of life and worship. Renewal should bring about responsive observances (communion), the unity and intelligent participation of the entire assembly. The renewal should serve the unity of believers (reconciliation) before, during, and after liturgy. The renewal must seek to embrace all of creation through proclamation. And as for the renewal, so for liturgical preparation. It should nurture Christian living, be the foundation for responsive observances, provide for the unity of believers. It should always embrace humanity.

When liturgies are prepared for the dignity and well-being of an entire assembly, *then* we will see the reconciliation we have known and treasured. *Then* we will fearlessly proclaim the Good News of peace and justice, promise and hope and redemption. *Then* we will be wheat milled and grapes crushed—in communion—so that we can see the hope of being one body, one Spirit in Christ. If we do not leave our gift and go, we may just as well have stayed home, because our remaining is a sham. Leave your gift and go. Actually, it is our dream.

Steadfast in Faith, Joyful in Hope, Untiring in Love: Preaching Everyday Mysteries

The prayers that we pray form us. This is no great bit of news that has not been promoted before. More to the point, preaching must lead us to believe that our faith has everything to do with our daily lives. Liturgy so often seems disconnected with life because for too long we have lived with the illusion that we must leave our lives outside the church doors when we enter into holy space. We have convinced ourselves that we have to become self-effacing in order to allow God to be strong and powerful, as though God needs that. Preaching the everyday mysteries recognizes that we are created in the image and likeness of God and have the possibility of knowing the fullness of God's love only when we come to a deep awareness of what being fully human means. When our faith is connected to everyday life, we are steadfast in faith, joyful in hope, untiring in love. The prayers that we pray form us.

The liturgical homily is the bridge between the paradigm of the Scriptures and the reality of human life. The preacher must know the language of the people so that the Scriptures can be understood by the hearers in such a way that true justice can be lived. Mary Catherine Hilkert has written, "The experience of grace is a communal experience. Hence the word of faith which the preacher proclaims is ultimately the community's word. The preacher speaks in the name of the community and speaks the deepest beliefs of the community."[1] As important as the scriptural text is, understanding the text of people's lives is absolutely critical in the homilist's task of crafting a message that can truly form the hearers. *Fulfilled In Your Hearing (FIYH)*, the United States Catholic Bishops' document on preaching, states, "Unless a preacher knows what a congregation needs, wants, or is able to hear, there is every possibility that the message offered in the homily will not meet the needs of the people who hear it."[2] To further elucidate the point, *FIYH* says, "If the homily must be faithful to the Scriptures for it to be the living Word of God, it must also be faithful to the congregation to whom this living Word of God is addressed."[3] As a liturgical act, then, the homily forms us as much as the prayers that we pray. In this way, the Word forms us to be "steadfast in faith, joyful in hope, untiring in love."[4] The homilist's task is to preach the everyday mysteries in the context of our public worship.

Thus, all homilies should make a statement of justice. All liturgical preaching uses the liturgy as the paradigm and context to address the Judeo-Christian expectation for right relationship with each other and with God. True justice preaching demands that we consider relationship with God and each other as part of the same act. When we are tempted to bifurcate Christ's command to love, the liturgy reminds us that love of God and love of neighbor are the same act. The justice preacher who weds the love of God and neighbor into one act has understood preaching as the fruit of true contemplation.

I recently read an article about pastoral ministry in an urban parish. The author states that in his life as a minister to the ministers, he has realized that he lives by the principles of con-

---

[1] Mary Catherine Hilkert, "Name Grace: A Theology of Proclamation," *Worship* (1986) 448.

[2] NCCB, *Fulfilled In Your Hearing: The Homily in the Sunday Assembly* (Washington, D.C.: USCC, 1982) 4.

[3] Ibid., 22.

[4] *The Roman Missal* (New York: Catholic Book Publishing Company, 1985). See solemn blessings of the first and third Sundays of Advent.

templative living: (1) Nothing will change, nor will anyone change, except me, if I submit to the process of living; (2) In everything, learn to live always without expectations; (3) Hold onto notion. What I hold onto too tightly will eventually be pried out of my fingers; (4) The goal of ministry is fidelity, not success; (5) In all things and at all times, do the best I can do; (6) Simply walk with God's people. Be a living presence of God; and (7) In all situations and at all times, love—no matter what happens, no matter what the cost.[5] While somewhat limited by lack of description, these principles remind us that preaching justice is not simply about changing behavior. Real justice preaching is an engagement in the art of letting go so that people are invited to live in right relationship. In this regard, the point of the homily is not to give moralistic answers, nor is it about coercion. Rather, the homily is to open people to the mysterious truths of conversion.

In his short story, "A Murder, A Mystery, and A Marriage," Mark Twain describes the Missouri farmer, John Gray, from the hamlet of Deer Lick:

> It was a straggling, drowsy hamlet of six or seven hundred inhabitants. These people knew, in a dim way, that out in the great world there were things called railways, steamboats, telegraphs and newspapers, but they had no personal acquaintance with them, and took no more interest in them than they did in the concerns of the moon. Their hearts were hogs and corn. The books used in the primitive village were more than a generation old; the aged Presbyterian minister, Rev. John Hurley, still dealt in the fire and brimstone of an obsolete theology; the very cut of the people's garments had not changed within the memory of any man.[6]

The homilist does not simply tell others what they must do to be just, but in a conversational manner, invites people to ask the probing questions so they can choose the good, so they can

[5] Joseph Diele, "Finding God in the City," *Human Development* (Winter 2000) 31.

[6] Mark Twain, "A Murder, A Mystery, and A Marriage," *The Atlantic Monthly* (July/August 2001) 54.

change their spiritual garments. The homily is never the place for moralizing. We know that lasting conversion is rooted in well-formed consciences that enable people to live authentic lives of virtue.

I can remember once being "cornered" at a casual party by a stranger who demanded to know what I was teaching students about preaching against abortion. I explained that I teach the same principles in regard to abortion that I teach in regard to doctor-assisted suicide, capital punishment, hate crimes, domestic violence, and abortion clinic bombers. My explanation was not well received! While recognizing that each of these justice issues has unique dimensions, preaching lays out the principles so that the hearer can come to reasonable assimilation of Church teaching. I have found that when people want a so-called "sample homily" written for a given occasion, the request is often for a ten-minute commercial that interrupts the liturgy and gives a moralistic conclusion. A true understanding of liturgical preaching flies in the face of such a request. And, though it is true that preaching always involves concreteness and specificity, good preaching will always lay the groundwork to address all of the various topics of justice.

For some reason, when we preach justice, we have numerous examples of preaching that seem to forget basic Christian anthropology, namely, that we are graced and, for all of our obvious instances of being tainted by sin, we are never characterized by those sins. *Imago Dei* is so essential to our character that we long for salvation, even if we do not know exactly for what we long. The imprint of God on each of us is undeniable, despite our tendency to convince ourselves otherwise.

This anthropological foundation places specific demands on the preacher. First, the preacher must trust the hearer. This necessitates that the preacher believes that the hearer will allow the preached Word to form him or her as the Spirit wills. Second, the preacher must truly believe that grace does abound. For all the evidence we have that sin and evil are a reality, God's grace is stronger, permeating all of human existence. Third, the preacher must long for the conversion of the hearer. When we allow the Word to confront, and not the preacher to confront, transformation into a more just way of life is possible.

Yes, the hearer is already on the road to conversion, but we know that his conversion is the journey of a lifetime—even into eternity.

These three guidelines for the preacher are always placed in a liturgical context when preaching justice. Especially when celebrating Eucharist, the primary sacramental statement of God's justice, the preacher determines what the rite itself is communicating. Because the entire liturgy preaches, the homilist can rely on the rite itself to carry the weight of conveying Christ's presence when our words may seem insufficient. And because every liturgical gathering is an event-in-time, the preacher must also plumb the ritual depths of the liturgy in which people are engaged. He or she must ask, What is the current experience of this time, this place? In this way, the liturgy itself becomes the hermeneutical lens through which people appropriate meaning. Contrary to some popular understandings about liturgy, we do not leave our real lives at the church doors so we can enter into a truly holy experience. Rather, we bring our lives, our world to worship with us and recognize the holiness that lies at its depth.

By way of example, the 2001 Holy Week brought ritual and preaching challenges in Cincinnati, Ohio. After a white police office shot and killed a black, unarmed man, riots and violence ensued. Curfews were imposed, necessitating schedule changes for Triduum celebrations. It was decided that since there could be no gatherings after dark within the city limits, the Easter Vigil would be canceled in all parish churches in the city. The rationale was that because darkness is integral to the celebration of the Easter Vigil, without darkness the integrity of the celebration would be compromised. A clear statement about liturgy was transmitted by the cancellation of the Easter Vigil. This was further emphasized as Catholics gathered on Easter Sunday to witness baptisms and receptions into the Church that normally would have been celebrated at the Vigil Mass.

There was also an added opportunity for preachers in the Cincinnati parishes to address real issues of justice on Easter Sunday. It would have been unconscionable to preach the resurrection without addressing issues of racism, classism, the necessity for peace and understanding in the face of acts of retaliation, as well as a host of other topics. Whether real or perceived, there were experiences of people not talking and listening to one another that had not been recognized. Consequently, tempers simmered and raged.

Preaching in these situations usually involves the sense and gift of prophecy. The prophet is not the person who has all the answers, or a crystal ball, or even an air of infallibility. Prophet-preachers are those people filled with such a love that they are also filled with a conviction to speak in such a manner that the vision of God becomes the vision of God's people. This challenges the preacher to be a person of prayer—and an active contemplative.

In preaching circles there is sometimes a desire to identify the preaching voices of our modern era to whom people listen. There is a sense of longing for the days when we had a Bishop Sheen, who broadly represented Catholicism. Who is the voice today? The answer, I believe, is that there cannot be that one voice today. As preaching moved from sermons to homilies, each particular congregation increasingly became the locus of the homiletic message. Preaching developed to find its power in addressing specific needs for specific people in specific places, with specific ways of hearing and appropriating the message. This dynamic challenges the preacher to realize that the use of the so-called homily helps might actually short-circuit the entire homiletic process because the resources are often too general for pastoral preaching. Specificity and concreteness became normative with the advent of homiletic preaching.

Today's preaching voices are those who preach week in and week out to people who are in relationship on an ongoing basis with the preacher, and vice versa. Justice preaching demands reflection on one's own life experiences in order to make the homiletic message understood with personal conviction. This is not simply a matter of sharing one's experience but uniting it with the experience of the community. Though the dimension of personal witness is important, the prophetic dimension of speaking for the Church and the people cannot be mitigated.

Richard Lischer, a homiletician from Duke University, recalls the time he traveled by train to his prep school in Wisconsin after Christmas vacation. The brakes on the train locked up, forcing all of the passengers to sit in a train station, where he and the other travelers intended to sleep until morning. At about 4:00 A.M. he was awakened by a middle-aged black man. "Excuse me," the man said politely. The man went on to explain that he and his wife were looking for his niece, who telephoned to say that her train got in late and she was in Chicago. The man did not realize that there were numerous train stations in Chicago. He asked Lischer to help search for the girl, to which Lischer agreed. The man realized that Lischer was headed toward Milwaukee, so he offered to drive Lischer there once they found the man's niece.

They began searching train stations, looking at people on benches and checking every restroom. They searched to no avail. The couple finally called their home in Milwaukee, where the niece for whom they were searching answered the phone. She had taken the bus home. So, the couple and Lischer left Chicago and headed toward Milwaukee. Lischer told his companion travelers that the searching had made him hungry. They agreed that it was time to eat and suggested that Lischer take their meal order, a remark that did not register with him at all. He wrote down their requests, went into a diner, and brought out the food. Other travelers in the area locked their cars, while Lischer ate breakfast with the black couple in their car. Only then did it dawn on him that prejudice prevented them from eating inside the restaurant. Lischer reflects:

> By the time we got to Milwaukee, it was a beautiful morning, and the circumstances of our breakfast had finally begun to register on me—me the unfinished product of segregated schools, churches, libraries, swimming pools, and restaurants. I had never eaten in a diner where the customer at the counter beside me was black. Never worshiped in a church where the Christian in the next pew was black. Never had a high school or college teacher who was black. Never a friend who was black. The banality of the arrangement was obvious. How routinely the Negro family incorporated this indignity into its daily system of life, like an old wound one learns to live with.[7]

---

[7] Richard Lischer, *Open Secrets: A Spiritual Journey Through a Country Church* (New York: Doubleday, 2001) 35.

Justice preaching addresses the old wounds that we have learned to live with. Each preacher addresses concrete situations of injustice, showing how God's grace transforms us to be more Christ-like in concrete, specific ways. We are indeed all unfinished products of prejudice, misinformation, and cruelty. Today's preaching voice, as it were, is the one who speaks to these concrete, specific instances. Our desire to have a sort of universal preacher is an unrealistic hope in a time when liturgical preachers gather with particular assemblies of faith.

As a liturgical act, then, a brief examination of how mystagogical preaching might help the preacher reveal everyday mysteries is in order. Characteristics for mystagogical preaching are outlined by Emily Besl and Jeff Kemper in six succinct points:

1. It makes concrete and specific references to the liturgical rite, words, gestures, actions, and structures.

2. It looks to Scripture for past instances or images of how God is working now in the liturgical act.

3. It connects the past, present, and future of salvation history so that the community's present liturgical act is seen in a wider context.

4. Implicit in mystagogical preaching is the doctrine of the Church.

5. It weaves the event-story-ritual-lived situation together; it is ultimately synthetic, not analytic (taking it apart and studying it).

6. It is not so much telling people how to live, as it is revealing the deep meaning of Christ's saving work in history and liturgy, which leads people to see differently, and thus live differently.[8]

The prayers that we pray form us. "Steadfast in faith, joyful in hope, untiring in love" is the heart of preaching a message of

---

[8] Taken from Pastoral Preaching website, sponsored by the Athenaeum of Ohio: <www.mtsm.org/preaching/index.htm>.

God's justice. Preaching as a liturgical act forms us in ways that sometimes comforts and sometimes disturbs. When the preacher preaches with love, the message always transforms.

To the best of my knowledge, I only have one letter of complaint in my official personnel file. The letter was addressed to the ordinary of my diocese; the writer was a visitor in the parish where I preached on Good Friday. The letter was pious in tone and chastised me for taking a political stand against capital punishment. I am not really sure, but the writer of the letter may have been correct on a number of points about the way I tried to open the Scriptures to the present world situation. But ten years later, three sentences remain with me: "Souls do not need political or social adjustment views from our Altars. We need to be led back to Jesus. We starve for spiritual food." The writer's conclusions were probably right; the premise was certainly wrong.

We *do* need political and social adjustment views when we worship. That is exactly what we need! To live justly is to recognize that our political and social views have everything to do with what we believe, and the way we live out those beliefs. Everything! How else will we be led back to Jesus? How else will our starving for spiritual food ever be realized?

R. Kevin Seasoltz, O.S.B.

Response to the Michael Mathis Award

On behalf of the monks of Saint John's Abbey who have published *Orate Fratres/Worship* since 1926, I am pleased to accept the Michael Mathis Award with gratitude and appreciation for the Center for Pastoral Liturgy and all that the Center has done for many years to promote life-giving liturgical celebrations in this country.

I would like to reflect for a few moments on my own brief association with Father Mathis. In the 1950s I was a diocesan seminarian at The Catholic University in Washington, D.C. While studying for a licentiate in sacred theology, I took five courses from the distinguished German patrologist Johannes Quasten. It was he who opened up for me the rich foundations of the Church's worship in the patristic period. With his encouragement, I applied for and was granted a summer scholarship in the graduate program in liturgical studies that Father Mathis had just established at Notre Dame.

I took a course on the history of liturgy from the Dutch liturgiologist Cornelius Bouman, a course on pastoral liturgy from Msgr. Martin Hellriegel, and a course on what was called "kerygmatic theology" from Johannes Hofinger, S.J. It was the latter course which made a significant difference in my life. At The Catholic University, I was being trained in what I usually experienced as rather sterile scholastic theology. Father Hofinger helped me see the essential relationships between theology and worship, theology and spirituality, and theology and life.

Shortly after ordination I was sent to the North American College in Rome to study canon law. While there I regularly worshiped on Sundays with the Benedictines at the College of Sant'Anselmo. That experience deepened by appreciation for the transcendence of God, the austere beauty of the Roman Rite, and the power of rituals executed with dignity and care. It was, however, a liturgy which was concerned almost exclusively with the worship of God but little or no reference to the joys and sorrows of people living in the city of Rome. I found the worship, nonetheless, deeply moving—so much so that I became a Benedictine shortly after my return to the States.

It was not until some years later that I encountered the life and writings of Dom Virgil Michel, a man whose horizons were broad and whose energies were spent not only in promoting the worship of God but also the transformation of human persons and communities. In the 1920s Father Virgil was sent by the abbot of Saint John's to study philosophy at Sant'Anselmo under the direction of Joseph Gredt. He found that experience quite suffocating, but he came to life on liturgical, ecumenical, and pastoral levels through his close association with Dom Lambert Beauduin, a Belgian monk of Mont César who taught fundamental theology at Sant'Anselmo. Beauduin had been instrumental in giving the modern liturgical movement in Europe a sound pastoral thrust.

Father Virgil brought the European liturgical movement to the United States but gave it a distinctively American character. His theology and pastoral sense were solidly grounded in the doctrine of the Mystical Body of Christ and a firm conviction that the liturgy belongs to the entire Church, not simply to clergy and religious, but to all lay men and women because through baptism they are all sons and daughters of God and sisters and brothers of Jesus Christ. In 1926 he established The Liturgical Press and began the publication of *Orate Fratres*. His understanding of the liturgy was reflected not only in the numerous articles he wrote but also in the other authors, both men and women, and the editorial advisors closely associated with *Orate Fratres*. As Nathan Mitchell pointed out in "The Amen Corner" for the January 2001 issue of *Worship*, one of the surprising things about the first volume of *Orate Fratres* is the significant presence of women among its authors. Likewise, he commented on the international character of issues discussed in that first volume. Another indication of Michel's vision is that he understood that the Church's liturgy is much broader than the Roman Rite. In concluding his column, Mitchell highlighted Michel's understanding of active and intelligent participation on the part of all the faithful, an understanding reflected in various articles from the first volume of the journal.

Father Virgil's horizons were far-reaching. He knew that the liturgical, social, educational, and biblical dimensions of the Church's life must be carefully interrelated. He also believed that rural and national political issues must be discussed in a liturgical context, because everything that touches on the life of the Mystical Body of Christ should be of concern to every worshiping Christian.

Father Virgil died suddenly in 1938, whereupon the editorship of the journal was assumed by Father Godfrey Diekmann, also a monk of Saint John's Abbey. Father Godfrey had been trained in theology at Sant'Anselmo but also spent a year at the Abbey of Maria Laach, the creative center of the liturgical movement in Germany. A popular lecturer and dynamic teacher, Father Godfrey served as editor of *Orate Fratres/Worship* for more than twenty-five years. He was one of the key figures in the North American Liturgical Conference during the 1940s and 1950s, a *peritus* at Vatican II, a very active member of the postconciliar Consilium for the implementation of the Roman Catholic liturgical reforms, and one of the founders of the International Commission on English in the Liturgy. It was under his direction that the name of the journal was changed from *Orate Fratres* to *Worship* in 1951–52. The change reflected the strong commitment of the editorial staff to the use of the vernacular in the liturgy so that all could participate actively and intelligently in the celebrations.

Between the years 1939 and 1954, the "Timely Tracts" written for the journal by H.A.R., Hans Ansgar Reinhold, surfaced in very challenging terms the major issues which were prominent in the minds of the leaders of the American liturgical movement. After H.A.R.'s death in 1968, Father Godfrey described him as "the pickerel in the American Catholic carp pond."

Especially useful during the years of the Second Vatican Council and its aftermath were the commentaries on the Constitution on the Sacred Liturgy and the newly revised Roman Catholic rites by Msgr. Frederick R. McManus, who combined historical and theological wisdom with a carefully nuanced hermeneutic of liturgical law.

In 1967 responsibility for editing *Worship* was assumed by Fathers Aelred Tegels and Michael Marx, both monks of Saint John's. Since numerous popular magazines and newsletters treated liturgical issues during and immediately after the Second Vatican Council, the new editors decided to emphasize the importance of liturgy for ecumenical encounter and to devote the journal to more scholarly articles. In an editorial announcement, Father Aelred noted that

> Growing interest in Orthodox theology and liturgy . . . has been an important factor in Catholic liturgical renewal. . . . Similarly, there is much to be gained for the continuing progress of liturgical renewal from a sympathetic study of the liturgical experience of the churches issuing from the Reformation and the vast and varied theological and liturgical literature in which this experience has found expression.[1]

Father Aelred regularly contributed "Chronicles" of liturgical developments, which were characterized by salty wit and a keen historical sense. Father Michael generally edited the articles, checked every footnote, exercised unerringly good judgment, and encouraged young scholars with his exquisite patience and kind corrections.

Beginning in 1983 until his sudden death in 1992, Robert Hovda enriched the pages of *Worship* with "The Amen Corner." A master pastoral liturgist, he had a great gift for discussing a wide variety of liturgical topics, but the Church as a community of the baptized was always at the center for his reflections. An often-cited paragraph from one of his *Worship* pieces on "The Vesting of Liturgical Ministers" captures both his style and the depth of his observations:

[1] *Worship* 41 (1967) 2.

> Good liturgical celebration, like a parable, takes us by the hair
> of our heads, lifts us momentarily out of the cesspool of in-
> justice we call home, puts us in the promised and challenging
> reign of God, where we are treated like we have never been
> treated anywhere else . . . where we are bowed to and sprinkled
> and censed and kissed and touched and where we share equally
> among all a holy food and drink.[2]

Since 1992 "The Amen Corner" has been written by Nathan D.
Mitchell, whose style is equally provocative, visionary, literary,
and wise. He is a gifted teacher whose life and writings are
equally sustained by poets, artists, theologians, and social
scientists.

It is not surprising that the various editors and authors who
have contributed so much to *Worship* have been honored over
the years with the Berakah Award by the North American
Academy of Liturgy: Godfrey Diekmann Frederick McManus,
Aelred Tegels, Michael Marx, Robert Hovda, Frank Kacmarcik,
and Nathan Mitchell.

In 1987 *Worship*'s editorial staff underwent another change;
I became the general editor, along with Fathers Aelred Tegels
and Allan Bouley as members of the editorial committee. Our
editorial policy has remained basically the same since 1967. As
I mentioned in a brief editorial notice in 1987:

> As worshiping communities continue to internalize the mean-
> ing of the extensive liturgical reforms that have taken place, to
> evaluate critically the effectiveness of those reformed and to
> search for new rituals that enable worshipers to praise and
> serve God amidst the rapidly changing cultural patterns in the
> world, we are convinced that we should continue to concentrate
> on a theoretic approach to liturgical issues. This does not mean
> that we shall not be concerned with practical matters. As ex-
> perience has shown, the doctrinal study of liturgy is often best
> situated at the level of concrete ritual structures and explicit
> pastoral problems.[3]

[2] *Worship* 54 (1980) 105.
[3] *Worship* 61 (1987) 80.

Worship continues to be professedly ecumenical. In fact the journal has never been narrowly confessional, as the members of the editorial board, the list of authors, and the subjects addressed in the journal indicate. It is concerned with the interface of Christianity and culture; it seeks to reflect on the role that the various theological disciplines, as well as the arts and social sciences, play in shaping Christian worship and the lives of worshiping Christians in the world.

The design and covers of the journal continue to be the work of Frank Kacmarcik, a claustral oblate of Saint John's. He has been responsible for the artistic presentation of the journal for over fifty years. His objective has been to provide readers not only with an intellectual experience but with an aesthetic experience as well. His hope is that the journal offers readers excellent examples of religious and liturgical art and design. Over the years, most of the artwork on the covers has been taken from his extraordinary collection of rare books, research books, prints and artifacts that he gathered and has given to Saint John's University under the name "Arca Artium." It consists of over four thousand rare books related to liturgy, over forty thousand research books in the areas of art and architecture, over four thousand original prints, and countless artifacts.

Worship is a juried periodical, which means that articles are generally not solicited; the content is dependent on articles freely submitted for consideration by the editors and consultants. In deciding which articles to publish, our challenge is to discern which topics need to be kept alive, which topics have been exhausted, and which topics simply need to be put on life support. For example, much more needs to be said about liturgical inculturation, the hermeneutics of liturgical law, the order for celebrating the sacraments of Christian initiation, liturgical spirituality and liturgical prayer, liturgy and social justice, the role of music and the other arts in the liturgy, the nature of eucharistic sacrifice, reconciliation, liturgical preaching, intercommunion, and the appropriation of lay men's and especially lay women's many gifts in the celebration of the liturgy, and of course, with just compensation for their ministry when that is appropriate. Discussions of the distinctive character of the ordained priesthood and vertical God-language, I think, have to be put on hold until there are significant breakthroughs in research and reflection on those topics. In general we do not publish articles that are exclusively historical because our readers are often not equipped to draw out the implications that such history has for contemporary celebrations. We think such articles are better placed in *Studia Liturgica, Ecclesia Orans,* and *Ephemerides Liturgicae.*

In the final analysis, a journal is only as good as the authors and articles that are published. In this regard, we are grateful for the many distinguished authors who over the years have submitted articles for publication. Included in that list are many faculty members and graduates of the programs in liturgical studies at Notre Dame.

Like many monastic projects, *Worship* has been quietly published out of a shoebox, with a very limited budget but with the help of many brothers. We have tried to dig deep into our Benedictine treasury of community life, prayer, and work. In the Benedictine tradition, we have a strong commitment to Scripture, liturgy, and the long but living tradition of the Church. We believe that liturgical theology, like all good theology, should be deeply rooted in tradition but situated not on the cutting edge, but rather on the growing edge. With God's gracious help and support from our many authors and subscribers, as editors of *Worship,* we hope we will continue to be faithful to our Benedictine motto: "Ut in omnibus glorificetur Deus"— "That in all things God may be glorified."

Contributors

Bro. David Andrews, C.S.C., is executive director of the National Catholic Rural Life Conference.

Walter J. Burghardt, S.J., is director of the "Preaching the Just Word" project at Woodstock Theological Center and professor emeritus at The Catholic University of America.

Tom East is coordinator of youth ministry services and the certificate program in youth ministry studies at the Center for Ministry Development.

Zeni Fox is associate professor of pastoral theology and director of the lay ministry program at Seton Hall University.

John P. Hogan retired as senior advisor in the Bureau of Educational and Cultural Affairs, U.S. State Department. Formerly he was Associate Director for International Operations at Peace Corps.

Eleanor M. Josaitis is cofounder and executive director of Focus: HOPE in Detroit, Michigan.

Msgr. William J. Linder is founder of New Community Corporation in Newark, New Jersey.

Daniel A. Lizárraga is associate director of the Secretariat for the Church in Latin America, United States Conference of Catholic Bishops.

Godfrey Mullen, O.S.B., is a monk of Saint Meinrad Archabbey and Ph.D. candidate in liturgical studies at The Catholic University of America.

Frances B. O'Connor, C.S.C., is adjunct professor at Holy Cross College, Notre Dame, Indiana. From 1990–97, she was guest scholar at the Kellogg Institute for International Studies at the University of Notre Dame.

Gilbert Ostdiek, O.F.M., is professor of liturgy at Catholic Theological Union and director of the Institute for Liturgical Consultants in Chicago.

Mary Alice Piil, C.S.J., is professor of liturgy at the Seminary of the Immaculate Conception, Huntington, New York.

John Roberto is founder and former director (1978–2000) of the Center for Ministry Development. Currently, he is the coordinator for CMD's Generations of Faith Project.

James M. Schellman is executive director of The North American Forum on the Catechumenate.

R. Kevin Seasoltz, O.S.B., is general editor of *Worship* and professor, Saint John's School of Theology • Seminary.

Del Staigers is pastor of Our Lady of Mercy Church in Dayton, Ohio. From 1991–2000, he taught at the Athenaeum of Ohio/Mount Saint Mary's Seminary, Cincinnati.

C. Vanessa White is director of the Augustus Tolton Pastoral Ministry Program and D. Min. candidate at Catholic Theological Union in Chicago.